Reteaching and Practice
Workbook

Grade 5

Scott Foresman·Addison Wesley

enVisionMATH®
Common Core

PEARSON

Glenview, Illinois • Boston Massachusetts • Chandler, Arizona • Upper Saddle River, New Jersey

ISBN-13: 978-0-328-69762-5

ISBN-10: 0-328-69762-1

9 10 V039 20 19 18 17 16 15 14

Contents

Name _____

Place Value

Place-value chart:

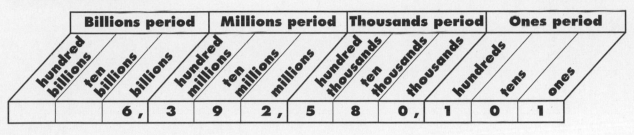

Billions period			Millions period			Thousands period			Ones period		
hundred billions	ten billions	billions	hundred millions	ten millions	millions	hundred thousands	ten thousands	thousands	hundreds	tens	ones
		6,	3	9	2,	5	8	0,	1	0	1

Expanded form: 6,000,000,000 + 300,000,000 + 90,000,000 + 2,000,000 + 500,000 + 80,000 + 100 + 1

Standard form: 6,392,580,101

Word form: six billion, three hundred ninety-two million, five hundred eighty thousand, one hundred one

---

Write the word name for each number and tell the value of the underlined digit.

1. 3,5<u>5</u>2,308,725

_____

_____

_____

2. <u>8</u>43,208,732,833

_____

_____

_____

_____

3. Write 2,000,000,000 + 70,000,000 + 100,000 + 70,000 + 3,000 + 800 + 10 in standard form.

_____

4. What number is 100,000,000 more than 5,438,724,022?

_____

Place Value

Write the word form for each number and tell the value of the underlined digit.

1. 34,23<u>5</u>,345

_____

_____

2. 1<u>9</u>,673,890,004

_____

_____

3. Write 2,430,090 in expanded form.

_____

Write each number in standard form.

4. 80,000,000 + 4,000,000 + 100 + 8   _____

5. twenty-nine billion, thirty-two million   _____

6. What number is 10,000 less than
337,676?   _____

7. Which number is 164,502,423 decreased by 100,000?

   A 164,402,423   **B** 164,501,423   **C** 164,512,423   **D** 264,502,423

8. Write 423,090,709,000 in word form.

_____

_____

_____

Name _____

Tenths and Hundredths

Fractions can also be named using decimals.

8 out of 10 sections are shaded.

The fraction is $\frac{8}{10}$.

The word name is eight tenths.

The decimal is 0.8.

Remember: the first place to the right of the decimal is tenths.

Write $\frac{2}{5}$ as a decimal.

Sometimes a fraction can be rewritten as an equivalent fraction that has a denominator of 10 or 100.

$$\frac{2}{5} = \frac{2 \times 2}{5 \times 2} = \frac{4}{10}$$

$$\frac{4}{10} = 0.4$$

So, $\frac{2}{5} = 0.4$.

Write $3\frac{3}{5}$ as a decimal.

First write the whole number.

3

Write the fraction as an equivalent fraction with a denominator of 10.

Change the fraction to a decimal.

$$\frac{3}{5} = \frac{3 \times 2}{5 \times 2} = \frac{6}{10} = 0.6$$

Write the decimal next to the whole number

3.6

So, $3\frac{3}{5} = 3.6$.

Write 0.07 as a fraction.

The word name for 0.07 is seven hundredths.

"Seven" is the numerator, and "hundredths" is the denominator.

So, $0.07 = \frac{7}{100}$.

Remember: the second place to the right of the decimal is hundredths.

Write each fraction or mixed number as a decimal.

1. $\frac{1}{5}$ _____   **2.** $\frac{6}{25}$ _____   **3.** $2\frac{3}{4}$ _____   **4.** $3\frac{9}{10}$ _____

Write each decimal as a fraction or mixed number.

5. 1.25 _____   **6.** 3.29 _____

7. 0.65 _____   **8.** 5.6 _____

9. Dan says $\frac{3}{5}$ is the same as 3.5. Is he correct? Explain.

_____

_____

Name _____

Tenths and Hundredths

Write a decimal and fraction for the shaded portion of each model.

1.   **2.**

_____   _____   _____   _____

Write each decimal as either a fraction or a mixed number.

3. 0.6 _____   **4.** 0.73 _____

5. 6.9 _____   **6.** 8.57 _____

Write each fraction or mixed number as a decimal.

7. $\frac{7}{10}$ _____   **8.** $\frac{33}{100}$ _____

9. $7\frac{2}{10}$ _____   **10.** $3\frac{9}{100}$ _____

Use division to change each fraction to a decimal.

11. $\frac{4}{5}$ _____   **12.** $\frac{12}{25}$ _____

13. $\frac{1}{50}$ _____   **14.** $\frac{11}{20}$ _____

15. When you convert 0.63 to a fraction, which of the following could be the first step of the process?

   A Since there are 63 hundredths, multiply 0.63 and 100.

   B Since there are 63 tenths, divide 0.63 by 10.

   C Since there are 63 tenths, place 63 over 10.

   D Since there are 63 hundredths, place 63 over 100.

Name _____

Thousandths

Example 1: Write 0.025 as a fraction.

Ones	.	Tenths	Hundredths	Thousandths
0	.	0	2	5

You can use a place-value chart to write a decimal as a fraction. Look at the place-value chart above. The place farthest to the right that contains a digit tells you the denominator of the fraction. In this case, it is thousandths. The number written in the place-value chart tells you the numerator of the fraction. Here, it is 25.

$0.025 = \frac{25}{1,000}$

Example 2: Write $\frac{11}{1,000}$ as a decimal.

Ones	.	Tenths	Hundredths	Thousandths
	.			

You can also use a place-value chart to write a fraction as a decimal. The denominator tells you the last decimal place in your number. Here, it is thousandths. The numerator tells you the decimal itself. Write a 1 in the hundredths place and a 1 in the thousandths place. Fill in the other places with a 0.

$\frac{11}{1,000} = 0.011$

Write each decimal as a fraction.

1. 0.002 _____   **2.** 0.037 _____   **3.** 0.099 _____

Write each fraction as a decimal.

4. $\frac{5}{1,000}$ _____   **5.** $\frac{76}{1,000}$ _____   **6.** $\frac{40}{1,000}$ _____

7. Matt reasoned that he can write $\frac{9}{1,000}$ as 0.9. Is he correct? Explain your answer.

_____

_____

Thousandths

Write each decimal as either a fraction or a mixed number.

1. 0.007 _____

2. 0.052 _____

3. 0.038 _____

4. 0.259 _____

5. 3.020 _____

6. 4.926 _____

Write each fraction as a decimal.

7. $\frac{73}{1,000}$ _____

8. $\frac{593}{1,000}$ _____

9. $\frac{854}{1,000}$ _____

10. $\frac{11}{1,000}$ _____

11. $\frac{5}{1,000}$ _____

12. $\frac{996}{1,000}$ _____

Write the numbers in order from least to greatest.

13. $\frac{5}{1,000}$, 0.003, $\frac{9}{1,000}$ _____

14. 0.021, 0.845, $\frac{99}{1,000}$ _____

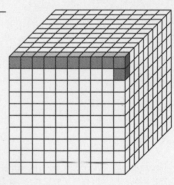

15. Look at the model at the right. Write a fraction and a decimal that the model represents.

_____

16. In Tasha's school, 0.600 of the students participate in a school sport. If there are one thousand students in Tasha's school, how many participate in a school sport?

A 6,000   **B** 600   **C** 60   **D** 6

17. Explain how knowing that $5 \div 8 = 0.625$ helps you write the decimal for $4\frac{5}{8}$.

_____

_____

Decimal Place Value

Here are different ways to represent 2.753.

Place-value chart:

Ones		Tenths	Hundredths	Thousandths
2	.	7	5	3

Expanded Form:

2 + 0.7 + 0.05 + 0.003

Standard form: 2.753

Word Form: Two and seven hundred fifty-three thousandths

Complete the place-value chart for the following number. Write its word form and tell the value of the underlined digit.

1. 6.3<u>2</u>4

Ones		Tenths	Hundredths	Thousandths
	.			

_____

_____

_____

Write each number in standard form.

2. 5 + 0.1 + 0.03 + 0.006

_____

3. Two and seven hundred twenty-four thousandths

_____

Decimal Place Value

Write the word form of each number and tell the value of the underlined digit.

1. 3.<u>1</u>00

_____

2. 5.2<u>6</u>7

_____

3. 2.77<u>8</u>

_____

Write each number in standard form.

4. 8 + 0.0 + 0.05 + 0.009

_____

5. 1 + 0.9 + 0.08 + 0.001

_____

Write two decimals that are equivalent to the given decimal.

6. 5.300   **7.** 3.7   **8.** 0.9

_____   _____   _____

9. The longest stem on Eli's
geranium plant is 7.24 inches.
Write 7.24 in word form.

_____

_____

10. The number 4.124 has two 4s.
Why does each 4 have a different
value?

_____

_____

_____

Comparing and Ordering Decimals

List the numbers in order from least to greatest:

6.943, 5.229, 6.825, 6.852, 6.779

Step 1: Write the numbers, lining up places. Begin at the left to find the greatest or least number.	Step 2: Write the remaining numbers, lining up places. Find the greatest and least. Order the other numbers.	Step 3: Write the numbers from least to greatest.
6.943 5.229 6.825 6.852 6.779 5.229 is the least.	6.943 ← greatest 6.825 ⌐ → 6.825 6.852 ⌐ → 6.852 6.779 ← least 6.779 is the least. 6.943 is the greatest. 6.852 is greater than 6.825.	5.229 6.779 6.825 6.852 6.943

Complete. Write >, <, or = for each ◯.

1. 7.539 ◯ 7.344   **2.** 9.202 ◯ 9.209   **3.** 0.75 ◯ 0.750

Order these numbers from least to greatest.

4. 3.898   3.827   3.779

_____

5. 5.234   5.199   5.002   5.243

_____

Which had the faster speed?

6. Driver A or Driver D

_____

7. Driver C or Driver A

_____

Car Racing Winners

Driver	Average Speed (mph)
Driver A	145.155
Driver B	145.827
Driver C	147.956
Driver D	144.809

Comparing and Ordering Decimals

Write >, <, or = for each ◯ .

1. 5.424 ◯ 5.343

2. 0.33 ◯ 0.330

3. 9.489 ◯ 9.479

4. 21.012 ◯ 21.01

5. 223.21 ◯ 223.199

6. 5.43 ◯ 5.432

Order these numbers from least to greatest.

7. 8.37, 8.3, 8.219, 8.129 _____

8. 0.012, 0.100, 0.001, 0.101 _____

9. Name three numbers between 0.33 and 0.34.

_____

10. Which runner came in first place?

_____

11. Who ran faster, Amanda or Steve?

_____

12. Who ran for the longest time?

_____

Half-Mile Run

Runner	Time (minutes)
Amanda	8.016
Calvin	7.049
Liz	7.03
Steve	8.16

13. Which number is less than 28.43?

A 28.435   B 28.34   C 28.430   D 29.43

14. Explain why it is not reasonable to say that 4.23 is less than 4.13.

_____

_____

_____

Name _____

Problem Solving: Look for a Pattern

Mr. Nagpi works in a machine shop. In the shop, the drill bits are kept in a cabinet with drawers. The drawers are marked with the diameter of the bits as shown on the right. Some of the labels are missing. Help Mr. Nagpi complete the drawer labels.

Drill Bits

0.10 in.	0.12 in.	0.14 in.	0.16 in.	0.18 in.
0.20 in.	0.22 in.	0.24 in.	0.26 in.	0.28 in.
0.30 in.	0.32 in.	0.34 in.		

Read and Understand

What do you know?

Some drawers are labeled with decimals.

What are you trying to find?

A way to find the values of the missing labels

Plan and Solve

Find a pattern for the decimals.

1. Look for a pattern to the change in the tenth-values across a row or down a column.

2. Look for a pattern to the change in the hundredth-values across a row or down a column.

3. Use the patterns to complete the table.

1. The tenth-values are not increasing across a row. They are increasing by 1 down a column.

2. The hundredth-values are increasing by 2 across a row. They are not increasing down a column.

3. The missing labels in the third row are 0.36 in. and 0.38 in.

Find the pattern in the table. Then fill in the missing values in the table.

0.20	0.21	0.22	0.23	0.24
0.50	0.51	0.52	0.53	
0.80	0.81	0.82		

Name _____

Problem Solving: Look for a Pattern

Determine the pattern and then complete the grids.

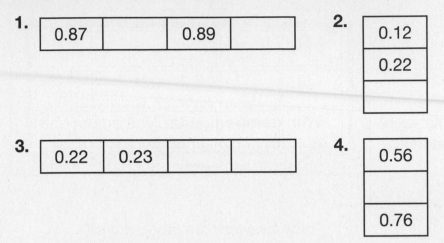

1.

0.87		0.89	

2.

0.12
0.22

3.

0.22	0.23		

4.

0.56
0.76

5. In a list of numbers, the pattern increases by 0.001 as you move to the right. If the third number in the list is 0.064, what is the first number in the list? Explain how you know.

_____

_____

6. If 5 school buses arrive, each carrying exactly 42 passengers, which expression would you use to show how many people in all arrived on the school buses?

A 42 + 5   **B** 42 − 5   **C** 42 × 5   **D** 42 ÷ 5

7. Mishell arranged her coins in the following pattern: $0.27, $0.29, $0.31, $0.33. Explain what her pattern is, and then tell what the next amount of coins would be.

_____

_____

Mental Math

There are several ways that you can add and subtract decimals mentally to solve a problem.

Commutative Property of Addition

You can add two decimal numbers in any order.

$$15.75 + 2.25 = 2.25 + 15.75$$

Associative Property of Addition

You can change the groupings of addends.

$$1.7 + (1.3 + 7) = (1.7 + 1.3) + 7$$

Compatible numbers are numbers that are easy to compute mentally.

$$2.6 + 9.3 + 7.4$$

2.6 and 7.4 are compatible because they are easy to add.

$$2.6 + 9.3 + 7.4 = (2.6 + 7.4) + 9.3$$
$$= 10 + 9.3 = 19.3$$

With **compensation**, you adjust one or both decimal numbers to make computations easier and compensate to get the final answer.

$$3.76 - 1.26$$
$$- .01 - .01$$
$$\downarrow \qquad \downarrow$$
$$3.75 - 1.25 = 2.5$$

Add or subtract mentally.

1. $16.9 + 12.1 =$ _____

2. $100.5 - 21.5 =$ _____

3. $8.01 + 1.09 =$ _____

4. $2.65 + 4.01 + 3.34 =$ _____

5. How much heavier is a Hippo than a Moose?

_____

Weight of Zoo Animals

Animal	Weight (Tons)
Hippo	2.5
Elephant	3.85
Rhino	2.15
Moose	.5

6. How heavy are the Elephant and the Rhino combined?

_____

7. What is the total weight of all four animals?

_____

Name _____

Mental Math

Show how you can use mental math to add or subtract.

1. $7.03 + 9.0 + 3.07 =$ _____

2. $63.75 - 13.25 =$ _____

Estimated Population in Millions

City	State	Population
San Antonio	Texas	1.4 million
Phoenix	Arizona	1.6 million
San Diego	California	1.3 million
Chicago	Illinois	2.7 million

3. How many more people live in
Phoenix than live in
San Antonio? _____

4. How many people live in San
Diego and Chicago combined? _____

5. A hotel bought 56.4 lb of apples in August from a local
orchard. In September, the hotel purchased an additional
52.34 lb of apples and 32.26 lb of strawberries. How many
pounds of fruit did the hotel buy?

    A 132 lbs   **B** 141 lbs   **C** 139 lbs   **D** 140.5 lbs

6. Explain It Write the definition and give an example of the
Commutative Property of Addition using decimal numbers.

_____

_____

_____

Rounding Whole Numbers and Decimals

You can use the number line below to help you round 8,237,650 to the nearest million. Is 8,237,650 closer to 8,000,000 or 9,000,000?

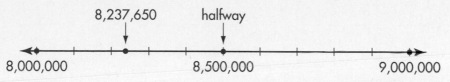

8,237,650 is less than halfway to 9,000,000. 8,237,650 is closer to 8,000,000.

The number line can also help you round 7.762 to the nearest tenth. Is 7.762 closer to 7.7 or 7.8?

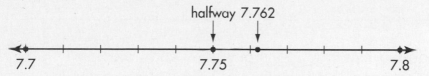

7.762 is more than halfway to 7.8. 7.762 is closer to 7.8.

Round each number to the place of the underlined digit.

1. 4,7̲25,806

2. 7̲.049

_____

_____

3. 1̲65,023,912

4. 18.6̲92

_____

_____

5. Round the number of connected computers in Year 2 to the nearest ten million.

_____

Number of Computers Connected to the Internet

Year 1	30,979,376
Year 2	42,199,279
Year 3	63,592,854

6. Marc earned $9.37 per hour working at the library. Round his wage to the nearest ten cents.

_____

Rounding Whole Numbers and Decimals

Round each number to the place of the underlined digit.

1. 32.<u>6</u>0 _____

2. 48<u>9</u>,334,209 _____

3. 32<u>4</u>,650 _____

4. 32.<u>0</u>73 _____

5. Name two different numbers that round to 30 when rounded to the nearest ten.

_____

In 2000, Italy produced 7,464,000 tons of wheat, and Pakistan produced 21,079,000 tons of wheat. Round each country's wheat production in tons to the nearest hundred thousand.

6. Italy _____

7. Pakistan _____

The price of wheat in 1997 was $3.38 per bushel. In 1998, the price was $2.65 per bushel. Round the price per bushel of wheat for each year to the nearest tenth of a dollar.

8. 1997 _____

9. 1998 _____

10. Which number rounds to 15,700,000 when rounded to the nearest hundred thousand?

   A 15,000,000   **B** 15,579,999   **C** 15,649,999   **D** 15,659,999

11. **Writing to Explain** Write a definition of rounding in your own words.

_____

_____

Estimating Sums and Differences

During one week, Mr. Graham drove a truck to five different towns to make deliveries. Estimate how far he drove in all.

Mr. Graham's Mileage Log

Cities	Mileage
Mansley to Mt. Hazel	243
Mt. Hazel to Perkins	303
Perkins to Alberton	279
Alberton to Fort Maynard	277
Fort Maynard to Mansley	352

To estimate the sum, you can round each number to the nearest hundred miles.

$$243 \Rightarrow 200$$
$$303 \Rightarrow 300$$
$$279 \Rightarrow 300$$
$$277 \Rightarrow 300$$
$$+352 \Rightarrow +400$$
$$1{,}500 \text{ mi}$$

Mr. Graham drove about 1,500 mi.

You can estimate differences in a similar way.

Estimate $7.25 - 4.98$.

You can round each number to the nearest whole number.

$$7.25 \Rightarrow 7$$
$$-4.98 \Rightarrow -5$$
$$2$$

The difference is about 2.

Estimate each sum or difference.

1. $19.7 - 6.9$

2. $59 + 43 + 95$

_____

_____

3. $582 + 169 + 23$

4. $87.99 - 52.46$

_____

_____

5. Estimation Brigid worked 16.75 h. Kevin worked 12.50 h. About how many more hours did Brigid work than Kevin?

_____

Estimating Sums and Differences

Estimate each sum or difference.

1. 5,602 − 2,344 _____

2. 7.4 + 3.1 + 9.8 _____

3. 2,314 + 671 _____

4. 54.23 − 2.39 _____

5. Wesley estimated 5.82 − 4.21 to be about 2. Is this an overestimate or an underestimate? Explain.

_____

_____

6. Estimate the total precipitation in inches and the total number of days with precipitation for Asheville and Wichita.

Average Yearly Precipitation of U.S. Cities		
City	Inches	Days
Asheville, North Carolina	47.71	124
Wichita, Kansas	28.61	85

_____

7. Which numbers should you add to estimate the answer to this problem: 87,087 + 98,000?

A 88,000 + 98,000

C 87,000 + 98,000

B 85,000 + 95,000

D 80,000 + 90,000

8. **Estimation** Estimate the total weight of two boxes that weigh 9.4 lb and 62.6 lb using rounding and compatible numbers. Which estimate is closer to the actual total weight? Why?

_____

_____

Modeling Addition and Subtraction of Decimals

Adding decimals using a hundredths grid:

Add 0.32 + 0.17.

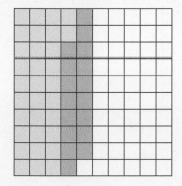

Step 1: Shade 32 squares to show 0.32.

Step 2: Use a different color. Shade 17 squares to show 0.17.

Step 3: Count all the squares that are shaded. How many hundredths are shaded in all? Write the decimal for the total shaded squares: 0.49.

So, 0.32 + 0.17 = 0.49.

Subtracting decimals using a hundredths grid:

Subtract 0.61 − 0.42.

Step 1: Shade 61 squares to show 0.61.

Step 2: Cross out 42 squares to show 0.42.

Step 3: Count the squares that are shaded but not crossed out. Write the decimal: 0.19.

So, 0.61 − 0.42 = 0.19.

Add or subtract. You may use hundredths grids to help.

1. 0.22 + 0.35 = _____

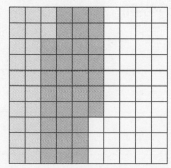

2. 0.52 − 0.41 = _____

Modeling Addition and Subtraction of Decimals

Add or subtract. Use hundredths grids if necessary.

1. 0.12 + 0.56 = _____

2. 0.27 − 0.09 = _____

3. 0.86 + 0.54 = _____

4. 1.27 + 0.75 = _____

5. 0.93 − 0.25 = _____

6. 1.07 − 0.61 = _____

7. 1.13 − 1.02 = _____

8. 0.28 + 1.96 = _____

9. Is the difference of 1.45 − 0.12 less than or greater than 1? _____

10. A bottle of nail polish holds 0.8 ounce. A bottle of perfume holds 0.45 ounce. How many more ounces does a bottle of nail polish hold? _____

11. Add: 1.18 + 1.86

  A 2.04   **B** 2.94   **C** 3.04   **D** 3.14

12. **Writing to Explain** Explain how to use hundredths grids to subtract 1.65 − 0.98.

_____

_____

_____

Name _____

Problem Solving: Draw a Picture and Write an Equation

A community center is raising funds to buy a computer. Here is a picture of the sign they put outside the center. How much more money must the center raise?

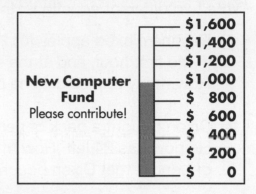

New Computer Fund
Please contribute!

—	$1,600
—	$1,400
—	$1,200
—	$1,000
—	$ 800
—	$ 600
—	$ 400
—	$ 200
—	$ 0

How to write an equation number sentence for a problem:

One Way

The goal is $1,600.

So far, $1,000 has been raised.

The amount yet to be raised is the unknown.

Think: The amount raised so far and the amount yet to be raised will reach the goal.

Write an equation.

$$1,000 + x = 1,600$$

Think: What number added to 1,000 will result in 1,600?

$$1,000 + \mathbf{600} = 1,600$$

The amount yet to be raised is $600.

Another Way

The goal is $1,600.

So far, $1,000 has been raised.

The amount yet to be raised is the unknown.

Think: The difference between the goal and what has been raised so far is the amount yet to be raised.

Write an equation.

$$1,600 - 1,000 = x$$

Think: What number will result if 1,000 is subtracted from 1,600?

$$1,600 - 1,000 = \mathbf{600}$$

The amount yet to be raised is $600.

A mason needs 22 bricks to make a stoop. So far he has carried 15 to the site. How many more bricks must he carry?

Draw a picture. Write an equation. Write a number sentence. Solve.

_____

Problem Solving: Draw a Picture and Write an Equation

Write two different equations; then solve each problem.

1. Dayana picked apples for 2 hours. She picked 28 apples in the first hour, and at the end of two hours, she had 49. How many apples did she pick during the second hour? _____

2. Dixon bought a pack of pencils and then gave 12 away. He now has 24 left. How many pencils were in the pack of pencils that Dixon bought? _____

Copy and complete the picture. Then write an equation and solve.

3. Rumina is baking 25 muffins for the bake sale. She has already baked 12. How many more does she need to bake?

25 muffins in all	
12	n

_____

4. **Estimation** Janet saved 22 dollars one month and 39 dollars the next month. She wants to buy a bicycle that costs $100. About how much more money does she need?

A about $40   B about $50   C about $60   D about $70

5. **Writing to Explain** Stefany ran 2 miles each day for 14 days. How many miles did she run in 14 days? Explain two different ways to solve this problem, and then solve.

_____

_____

Adding Decimals

In February, Chantell ran a 5K race in 0.6 hour. She ran another 5K race in May in 0.49 hour. What was her combined time for the two races?

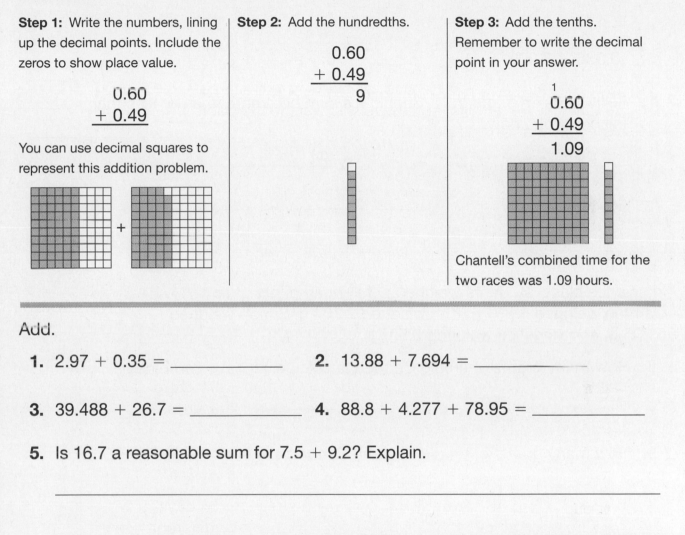

Step 1: Write the numbers, lining up the decimal points. Include the zeros to show place value.

$$
\begin{array}{r}
0.60 \\
+\ 0.49 \\
\hline
\end{array}
$$

You can use decimal squares to represent this addition problem.

Step 2: Add the hundredths.

$$
\begin{array}{r}
0.60 \\
+\ 0.49 \\
\hline
9
\end{array}
$$

Step 3: Add the tenths. Remember to write the decimal point in your answer.

$$
\begin{array}{r}
{}^{1}\ \ \ \\
0.60 \\
+\ 0.49 \\
\hline
1.09
\end{array}
$$

Chantell's combined time for the two races was 1.09 hours.

Add.

1. 2.97 + 0.35 = _____

2. 13.88 + 7.694 = _____

3. 39.488 + 26.7 = _____

4. 88.8 + 4.277 + 78.95 = _____

5. Is 16.7 a reasonable sum for 7.5 + 9.2? Explain.

_____

_____

6. How much combined snowfall was there in Milwaukee and Oklahoma City?

_____

City	Snowfall (inches) in 2000
Milwaukee, WI	87.8
Baltimore, MD	27.2
Oklahoma City, OK	17.3

Name _____

Adding Decimals

Add.

1.	58.0 + 3.6	2.	40.5 + 22.3	3.	34.587 + 21.098	4.	43.1000 + 8.4388

5. 16.036 + 7.009 = _____

6. 92.30 + 0.32 = _____

7. Reilly adds 45.3 and 3.21. Should his sum be greater than or less than 48? Tell how you know.

_____

_____

_____

In science class, students weighed different amounts of tin. Carmen weighed 4.361 g, Kim weighed 2.704 g, Simon weighed 5.295 g, and Angelica weighed 8.537 g.

8. How many grams of tin did Carmen and Angelica have combined?

_____

9. How many grams of tin did Kim and Simon have combined?

_____

10. In December the snowfall was 0.03 in. and in January it was 2.1 in. Which was the total snowfall?

A 3.2 in.   **B** 2.40 in.   **C** 2.13 in.   **D** 0.03 in.

11. Writing to Explain Explain why it is important to line up decimal numbers by their place value when you add or subtract them.

_____

_____

_____

Subtracting Decimals

Mr. Montoya bought 3.5 lb of ground beef. He used 2.38 lb to make hamburgers. How much ground beef does he have left?

Step 1: Write the numbers, lining up the decimal points. Include the zeros to show place value.

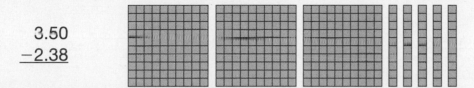

```
  3.50
- 2.38
```

You can use decimal squares to represent this subtraction problem.

Step 2: Subtract the hundredths. Regroup if you need to.

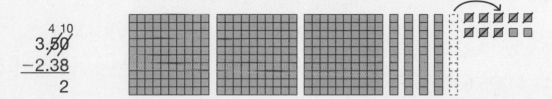

```
    4 10
  3.5̶0̶
- 2.38
      2
```

Step 3: Subtract the tenths and the ones. Remember to write the decimal point in your answer.

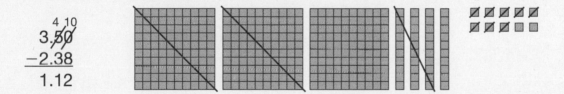

```
    4 10
  3.5̶0̶
- 2.38
  1.12
```

Mr. Montoya has 1.12 lb of ground beef left over.

Subtract.

1.   82.7
       − 5.59
    _____

2.   43.3
       − 12.82
    _____

3.   7.28
       − 4.928
    _____

Subtracting Decimals

Subtract.

| 1. | 92.1
 − 32.6 | 2. | 52.7
 − 36.9 | 3. | 85.76
 − 12.986 | 4. | 32.7
 − 2.328 |

5. 8.7 − 0.3 = _____   **6.** 23.3 − 1.32 = _____

7. Kelly subtracted 2.3 from 20 and got 17.7. Explain why this answer is reasonable.

_____

_____

At a local swim meet, the second-place swimmer of the 100-m freestyle had a time of 9.33 sec. The first-place swimmer's time was 1.32 sec faster than the second-place swimmer. The third-place time was 13.65 sec.

8. What was the time for the first-place swimmer?   _____

9. What was the difference in time between the second- and third-place swimmers?   _____

10. Miami's annual precipitation in 2000 was 61.05 in. Albany's was 46.92 in. How much greater was Miami's precipitation than Albany's?

A 107.97 in.   **B** 54.31 in.   **C** 14.93 in.   **D** 14.13 in.

11. Writing to Explain Explain how to subtract 7.6 from 20.39.

_____

_____

_____

_____

_____

Name _____

Problem Solving:
Multiple-Step Problems

Kim has a $10 bill, a $20 bill, and 2 $5 gift certificates. She uses
the gift certificates toward the purchase of a CD for $14.00. How
much money does Kim have left after buying the CD?

Read and Understand

What do you know?

Kim has a ten-dollar bill, a twenty-dollar
bill, and two five-dollar gift certificates.

She uses the 2 certificates toward the
purchase of a CD that costs $14.00.

What are you trying to find?

How much money does Kim have left after
she buys the CD?

Plan and Solve

Answer these hidden questions.

How much money does Kim have?

$20.00 + $10.00 = $30.00

How much are the two
certificates worth?

$5.00 + $5.00 = $10.00

How much cash will Kim need to
buy the CD?

$14.00 − $10.00 = $4.00

Solve the problem.

Money − cash paid for CD = Money left
$30.00 − $4.00 = $26.00

Write the answer in a
complete sentence.

Kim has $26 left after buying the CD.

Look Back and Check

Is your answer correct?

Yes, $4.00 + $26.00 = $30.00

1. You can also find how much money Kim has left by
completing the following expression.

$10.00 + $20.00 + $5.00 + $5.00 − _____

Problem Solving: Multiple-Step Problems

Solve.

1. Theater tickets for children cost $5. Adult tickets cost $3 more. If 2 adults and 2 children buy theater tickets, what is the total cost?

   _____

2. Luis has a $10 bill and three $5 bills. He spends $12.75 on the entrance fee to an amusement park and $8.50 on snacks. How much money does he have left?

   _____

3. Alexandra earns $125 from her paper route each month, but she spends about $20 each month on personal expenses. To pay for a school trip that costs $800, about how many months does she need to save money? Explain.

   _____

   _____

4. Patty is a member of the environmental club. Each weekday, she volunteers for 2 hours. On Saturday and Sunday, she volunteers 3 hours more each day. Which expression shows how to find the number of hours she volunteers in one week?

   A $2 + 5$

   B $2 + 2 + 2 + 2 + 2 + 5 + 5$

   C $2 + 2 + 2 + 3 + 3$

   D $2 + 3 + 3$

5. Marco's goal is to eat only 2,000 calories each day. One day for breakfast he consumed 310 calories, for lunch he consumed 200 more calories than breakfast, and for dinner he consumed 800. Did he make his goal? Explain.

   _____

Name _____

Multiplication Properties

You can use multiplication properties to help you multiply more easily.

Associative Property of Multiplication
You can change the grouping of the factors. The product stays the same.

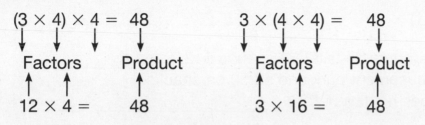

$(3 \times 4) \times 4 = 48$ $3 \times (4 \times 4) = 48$

Factors   Product   Factors   Product

$12 \times 4 = \quad 48$ $3 \times 16 = \quad 48$

Commutative Property of Multiplication
You can change the order of the factors. The product stays the same.

$7 \times 4 = \quad 28$ $4 \times 7 = \quad 28$

Factors   Product   Factors   Product

Zero Property of Multiplication
When one of the factors is 0, the product is always 0.

$3 \times 0 = \quad 0$ $0 \times 3 = \quad 0$

Factors   Product   Factors   Product

Identity Property of Multiplication
When one of the factors is 1, the product is always the other factor.

Identify the multiplication property or properties used in each equation.

1. $100 \times 0 = 0$ _____

2. $7 \times 2 = 2 \times 7$ _____

3. $1 \times 55 = 55$ _____

4. $(6 \times 7) \times 9 = 6 \times (7 \times 9)$ _____

Use the multiplication properties to determine what number must be in the box.

5. $5 \times 4 = \boxed{} \times 5$

6. $99 \times \boxed{} = 99$

7. $(3 \times 12) \times \boxed{} = 3 \times (12 \times 8)$

8. $\boxed{} \times 1 = 0$

9. $\boxed{} \times 2 = 2 \times 50$

10. $(16 \times \boxed{}) \times 25 = 16 \times (33 \times 25)$

R 3·1

Name _____

Multiplication Properties

In **1** through **5**, write the multiplication property used in each equation.

1. $53 \times 6 = 6 \times 53$ _____

2. $0 \times 374{,}387 = 0$ _____

3. $5 \times (11 \times 4) = (5 \times 11) \times 4$ _____

4. $42 \times 1 = 42$ _____

5. $14 \times 5 = 5 \times 14$ _____

6. Chan bought 2 large frozen yogurts at $1.50 each and 1 small bottle of water for $1.00. How much did she pay in total?

_____

7. Dan has 4 shelves. He has exactly 10 books on each shelf. Judy has 10 shelves. She has exactly 4 books on each shelf. Who has more books? Explain.

_____

_____

8. If $3 \times 8 \times 12 = 8 \times 3 \times n$, what is the value of *n*?

A 3   **B** 8   **C** 12   **D** 18

9. Write a definition for the Associative Property of Multiplication in your own words and explain how you would use it to compute $4 \times 25 \times 27$ mentally.

_____

_____

_____

Using Mental Math to Multiply

You can also use patterns to multiply mentally.

Fact: $6 \times 8 = \mathbf{48}$

$60 \times 8 = \mathbf{48}0$	$6 \times 80 = \mathbf{48}0$
$600 \times 8 = \mathbf{4,8}00$	$60 \times 80 = \mathbf{4,8}00$
$6,000 \times 8 = \mathbf{48,}000$	$600 \times 80 = \mathbf{48,}000$
$60,000 \times 8 = \mathbf{480,}000$	$6,000 \times 80 = \mathbf{480,}000$

Pattern: Notice that the product is always the digits 48 followed by the total number of zeros that are in the factors.

Find $30 \times 3 \times 50$.

Use the Commutative and Associative Properties of Multiplication to regroup.

$(30 \times 50) \times 3$

$1,500 \times 3 = 4,500$

Commutative Property of Multiplication	Associative Property of Multiplication
You can multiply factors in any order. $15 \times 9 = 9 \times 15$	You can change the grouping of factors. $(8 \times 20) \times 5 = 8 \times (20 \times 5)$

Find each product. Use patterns and properties to compute mentally.

1. $80 \times 90 =$ _____

2. $40 \times 800 =$ _____

3. $5 \times 10 \times 20 =$ _____

4. $4 \times 30 \times 25 =$ _____

5. You know that $6 \times 7 = 42$. How can you find 60×700?

_____

_____

_____

Using Mental Math to Multiply

Use mental math to find each product.

1. 150 × 20 =

_____

2. 0 × 50 × 800 =

_____

3. 500 × 40 =

_____

4. 120 × 50 =

_____

5. 60 × 70 × 1 =

_____

6. 9,000 × 80 =

_____

7. 100 × 10 × 1=

_____

8. 1,800 × 20 × 0 =

_____

9. 30 × 20 =

_____

10. 1,400 × 2,000 =

_____

11. 7,000 × 50 × 1 =

_____

12. 1,000 × 200 × 30 =

_____

13. A googol is a large number that is the digit one followed by one hundred zeros. If you multiply a googol by 100, how many zeros will that product have?

_____

14. Gregorios drives 200 miles per day for 10 days. How many miles did he drive in all?

_____

15. If $a \times b \times c = 0$, and a and b are integers greater than 10, what must c equal?

A 0   **B** 1   **C** 2   **D** 10

16. SungHee empties her piggy bank and finds that she has 200 quarters, 150 dimes, and 300 pennies. How much money does she have? Explain.

_____

_____

Estimating Products

A bus service drives passengers between Milwaukee and Chicago every day. They travel from city to city a total of 8 times each day. The distance between the two cities is 89 mi. In the month of February, there are 28 days. The company's budget allows for 28,000 total miles for February. Is 28,000 mi a reasonable budget mileage amount?

One Way to Estimate

Estimate 28 × 8 × 89.

Use rounding.

You can round 89 to 100 and 8 to 10. Then multiply.

28 × 10 × 100 = 280 × 100 = 28,000

Because this is an overestimate, there are enough miles.

Another Way to Estimate

Estimate 28 × 8 × 89.

Use compatible numbers.

Replace 28 with 30, 89 with 90, and 8 with 10. 30, 90, and 10 are compatible numbers because they are close to the actual numbers in the problem and they are easier to multiply. Now the problem becomes 30 × 90 × 10.

30 × 90 = 2,700   Multiply 3 × 9, then place two zeros after the product.

2,700 × 10 = 27,000   Multiply 27 × 1 using the Identity Property of Multiplication, then place three zeros after the product.

In the estimate, we used numbers greater than the original numbers, so the answer is an overestimate.

28,000 total miles is a reasonable budget amount.

Estimate each product. Use rounding or compatible numbers.

1. 42 × 5 × 90 = _____

2. 27 × 98 × 4 = _____

Mrs. Carter ordered new supplies for Memorial Hospital.

3. About how much will it cost to purchase 48 electronic thermometers?

_____

4. About how much will it cost to purchase 96 pillows?

_____

Supplies	
Electronic thermometers	$19 each
Pulse monitors	$189 each
Pillows	$17 each
Telephones	$19 each

Name _____

Estimating Products

Estimate each product.

1. 68 × 21 =

_____

2. 5 × 101 =

_____

3. 151 × 21 =

_____

4. 99 × 99 =

_____

5. 87 × 403 =

_____

6. 19 × 718 =

_____

7. 39 × 51 =

_____

8. 47 × 29 × 11 =

_____

9. 70 × 27 =

_____

10. 69 × 21 × 23 =

_____

11. 7 × 616 =

_____

12. 8,880 × 30 =

_____

13. Give three numbers whose product is about 9,000.

_____

Electronics Prices	
CD player	$ 74.00
MP3 player	$ 99.00
CD/MP3 player	$199.00
AM/FM radio	$ 29.00

14. About how much would it cost to buy 4 CD/MP3 players and 3 MP3 players?

_____

15. Which is the closest estimate for the product of 2 × 19 × 5?

A 1,150   **B** 200   **C** 125   **D** 50

16. Explain how you know whether an estimate of a product is an overestimate or an underestimate.

_____

_____

_____

Name _____

Exponents

You can use exponential notation to write a number that is being multiplied by itself.

There are two parts in exponential notation. The **base** tells you what factor is being multiplied. The **exponent** tells you how many of that factor should be multiplied together. The exponent is *not* a factor.

exponent

↓

$8^2 = 8 \times 8$ The base is 8, so 8 is the factor to be multiplied.
↑   The exponent is 2, so 2 factors of 8 should be
                     multiplied together.

base

You can write 8^2 in two other forms.

In **expanded** form, you write out your factors. Since 8^2 means you multiply two factors of 8, 8^2 in expanded form is 8×8.

In **standard** form, you write down the product of the factors. Since $8 \times 8 = 64$, 64 is the standard form of 8^2.

Write in exponential notation.

1. $2 \times 2 \times 2$ _____

2. $6 \times 6 \times 6 \times 6 \times 6$ _____

Write in expanded form.

3. 1^4 _____

4. 5^3 _____

Write in standard form.

5. $2 \times 2 \times 2 \times 2$ _____

6. 8^3 _____

7. A used car lot has 9 lanes for cars and 9 rows for cars in each lane. What is the exponential notation for the number of spaces on the lot? Can the owner fit 79 cars on the lot?

_____

Name _____

Exponents

For questions **1–4**, write in exponential notation.

1. $13 \times 13 \times 13$ _____

2. $8 \times 8 \times 8 \times 8 \times 8 \times 8$ _____

3. 64×64 _____

4. $4 \times 4 \times 4 \times 4$
$\times 4 \times 4 \times 4 \times 4$ _____

For questions **5–8**, write in expanded form.

5. 2^5 _____

6. 20 squared _____

7. 11^4 _____

8. 9 cubed _____

For questions **9–12**, write in standard form.

9. $4 \times 4 \times 4$ _____

10. 14 squared _____

11. 6^5 _____

12. $9 \times 9 \times 9 \times 9$ _____

13. Which of these numbers, written in expanded form, is equal
to 625?

    A $5 \times 5 \times 5 \times 5$

    B 5×5

    C $5 \times 5 \times 5$

    D $5 \times 5 \times 5 \times 5 \times 5$

14. Find the number equal to 6 raised to the second power.

    A 18

    B 36

    C 6

    D 12

15. Explain what 4 raised to the fourth power means.

_____

_____

P 3·4

Distributive Property

Hector's rock collection is in 7 cases. Each case holds 28 rocks.
How many rocks are in Hector's collection? You can use the
Distributive Property to find the product of 7 × 28.

Step 1. Split 28 into 20 + 8.
$7 \times 28 = 7 \times (20 + 8)$

Step 2. Multiply 7 times each part of
the sum.
$(7 \times 20) + (7 \times 8)$

$140 + 56$

Step 3. Use addition to find the sum.
$140 + 56 = 196$

OR Step 1. Split 28 into 30 − 2.
$7 \times 28 = 7 \times (30 - 2)$

Step 2. Multiply 7 times each part of
the difference.
$(7 \times 30) - (7 \times 2)$

$210 - 14$

Step 3. Use subtraction to find the
difference.
$210 - 14 = 196$

So, 7 × 28 = 196. Hector has 196 rocks in his collection.

Rewrite using the Distributive Property. Then find the product.

1. 3 × 42 _____

2. 39 × 5 _____

3. 6 × 147 _____

4. 19 × 70 _____

5. 54 × 67 _____

6. 90 × 83 _____

7. 364 × 26 _____

8. 45 × 678 _____

For questions **9** through **12**, find the value of *n*.

9. $4 \times 62 = (4 \times n) + (4 \times 2)$ _____

10. $79 \times 20 = (80 \times 20) - (n \times 20)$ _____

11. $53 \times 118 = (53 \times 100) + (n \times 18)$ _____

12. $352 \times 75 = (n \times 75) + (50 \times 75) + (2 \times 75)$ _____

13. Joey's class is collecting food for the school canned food
drive. There are 28 children in Joey's class. Each child
brought in 15 cans of food. Use the Distributive Property to
find out how many cans of food Joey's class collected.

_____

Name _____

Distributive Property

Use the Distributive Property to multiply mentally.

1. $5 \times 607 =$ _____

2. $16 \times 102 =$ _____

3. $7 \times 420 =$ _____

4. $265 \times 5 =$ _____

5. $44 \times 60 =$ _____

6. $220 \times 19 =$ _____

7. $45 \times 280 =$ _____

8. $341 \times 32 =$ _____

9. Fill in the blanks to show how the Distributive Property can be used to find 10×147.

$10 \times (150 - 3) = (10 \times 150) - ($_____ $\times 3) =$

$1,500 -$ _____ $=$ _____

10. In 1990, there were 1,133 tornadoes in the U.S. If there were the same number of tornadoes for 10 years in a row, what would be the 10-year total?

_____

11. There were 1,071 tornadoes in the U.S. in 2000. What is the number of tornadoes multiplied by 20?

_____

12. If $4 \times 312 = 4 \times 300 + n$, which is the value of n?

A 4   **B** 12   **C** 48   **D** 300

13. Margaret said that she used the Distributive Property to solve 4×444. Is her answer shown below correct? Explain.

$4 \times 444 = 4 \times (400 + 40 + 4) =$
$(4 \times 400) + (4 \times 40) + (4 \times 4) =$
$1,600 + 160 + 16 = 1,776$

_____

_____

Multiplying by 1-Digit Numbers

Mr. McGuire drives his truck 275 miles each day. How far does he drive in 3 days?

Find 275 × 3.

Step 1: Multiply the ones. Regroup if necessary.	**What You Think** 3 × 5 ones = 15 ones Regroup 15 ones as 1 ten and 5 ones.		**What You Write** 1 275 × 3 ——— 5
Step 2: Multiply the tens. Regroup if necessary.	**What You Think** 3 × 7 tens = 21 tens 21 tens + 1 ten = 22 tens Regroup as 2 hundreds and 2 tens.		**What You Write** 2 1 275 × 3 ——— 25
Step 3: Multiply the hundreds. Regroup if necessary.	**What You Think** 3 × 2 hundreds = 6 hundreds 6 hundreds + 2 hundreds = 8 hundreds No need to regroup.		**What You Write** 2 1 275 × 3 ——— 825

Mr. McGuire drives 825 miles in 3 days.

Find each product. Estimate to check that your answer is reasonable.

1. 31 × 7 _____
2. 29 × 4 _____
3. 88 × 6 _____

4. 25 × 9 _____
5. 102 × 8 _____
6. 211 × 7 _____

7. 552 × 3 _____
8. 471 × 9 _____
9. 73 × 4 _____

10. 266 × 8 _____
11. 390 × 2 _____
12. 514 × 6 _____

13. **Estimation** Estimate the product of 48 and 7. Do you have an underestimate or overestimate?

_____

_____

Name _____

Multiplying by 1-Digit Numbers

Find each product. Estimate to check that your answer is reasonable.

1. $58 \times 3 =$ _____   **2.** $49 \times 8 =$ _____

3. $83 \times 5 =$ _____   **4.** $95 \times 6 =$ _____

5. $273 \times 4 =$ _____   **6.** $35 \times 8 =$ _____

7. $789 \times 6 =$ _____   **8.** $643 \times 7 =$ _____

9.   68
    $\times\ 2$

10.   582
    $\times\ 5$

11.   84
    $\times\ 4$

12.   926
    $\times\ 7$

13. Xavier painted five portraits and wants to sell them for 36 dollars each. How much money will he make if he sells all five? _____

14. A farmer wants to build a square pigpen. The length of one side of the pen is 13 ft. How many feet of fencing should the farmer buy? _____

15. Jasmine wants to buy 4 green bags for 18 dollars each and 3 purple bags for 15 dollars each. She has 100 dollars. How much more money does she need? _____

16. A regular octagon is a figure that has eight sides with equal lengths. If one side of a regular octagon is 14 inches long, what is the perimeter of the entire octagon?

A 148 in.   **B** 140 in.   **C** 112 in.   **D** 84 in.

17. Why is 2,482 not a reasonable answer for 542×6?

_____

_____

_____

Multiplying 2-Digit by 2-Digit Numbers

Find 43 × 26.

Step 1:	**What You Think**	**What You Write**
Multiply by the ones.	6 × 3 ones = 18 ones	
Regroup if necessary.	Regroup 18 ones as 1 ten	1
	and 8 ones.	43
		× 26
	6 × 4 tens = 24 tens	258
	24 tens + 1 ten = 25 tens	
	Regroup 25 tens as 2 hundreds	
	and 5 tens.	
Step 2:	**What You Think**	1
Multiply by the tens.	20 × 3 ones = 60 ones	43
Regroup if necessary.	Regroup 60 ones as 6 tens.	× 26
		258
	20 × 4 tens = 80 tens	**860**
	Regroup 80 tens as 8 hundreds.	
Step 3:	**What You Think**	1
Add the partial products.	6 × 43 = 258	43
	20 × 43 = 860	× 26
		258 ← partial
		+ 860 ← products
		1,118

Find the product.

1.	38 × 12	**2.**	64 × 33	**3.**	49 × 27	**4.**	85 × 15
5.	26 × 21	**6.**	73 × 19	**7.**	57 × 28	**8.**	91 × 86

9. In the problem 62 × 45, what are the partial products?

_____

Name _____

Multiplying 2-Digit by 2-Digit Numbers

Find each product. Estimate to check that your answer is reasonable.

1. $\begin{array}{r} 56 \\ \times\ 34 \\ \hline \end{array}$

2. $\begin{array}{r} 45 \\ \times\ 76 \\ \hline \end{array}$

3. $\begin{array}{r} 35 \\ \times\ 15 \\ \hline \end{array}$

4. $\begin{array}{r} 47 \\ \times\ 94 \\ \hline \end{array}$

5. $\begin{array}{r} 64 \\ \times\ 51 \\ \hline \end{array}$

6. $\begin{array}{r} 47 \\ \times\ 30 \\ \hline \end{array}$

7. $\begin{array}{r} 56 \\ \times\ 19 \\ \hline \end{array}$

8. $\begin{array}{r} 92 \\ \times\ 49 \\ \hline \end{array}$

9. To pay for a sofa, Maddie made a payment of 64 dollars each month for one year. How much did the sofa cost ?

_____

10. Katie is in charge of buying juice for the teachers' breakfast party. If one teacher will drink between 18 and 22 ounces of juice, and there are 32 teachers, which is the best estimate for the amount of juice Katie should buy?

   A about 200 ounces

   B about 400 ounces

   C about 600 ounces

   D about 800 ounces

11. Is 7,849 a reasonable answer for 49×49? Why or why not?

_____

_____

_____

Name _____

Multiplying Greater Numbers

Find 128 × 23.   Estimate: 100 × 20 = 2,000

Step 1	Step 2	Step 3
Multiply by the ones. Regroup as needed.	Multiply by the tens. Regroup as needed.	Add the products.

```
                    2              1
    128            128            128
 ×   23          ×   3          ×  20
    1
    384    ←      384           2,560
 + 2,560   ←
    2,944  ←
```

Because the answer is close to the estimate, the answer is reasonable.

Find the product. Estimate to check if your answer is reasonable.

Problem	Multiply by the Ones	Multiply by the Tens	Add the Products
1. 282 × 19 2,538 ← + _____	7 1 282 × 9 2,538	282 × 10	
2. 538 × 46			

3. Is 2,750 a reasonable answer for 917 × 33? Explain.

_____

_____

_____

Name _____

Multiplying Greater Numbers

Find each product. Estimate to check that your
answer is reasonable.

1.   556
     $\times\ 34$

2.   234
     $\times\ 75$

3.   395
     $\times\ 76$

4.   483
     $\times\ 57$

5.   628
     $\times\ 33$

6.   154
     $\times\ 35$

7.   643
     $\times\ 49$

8.   536
     $\times\ 94$

9. In a class of 24 students, 13 students sold over 150 raffle tickets each, and
the rest of the class sold about 60 raffle tickets each. The class goal was to
sell 2,000 tickets. Did they reach their goal? Explain.

_____

_____

_____

10. Player A's longest home run distance is 484 ft.
If Player A hits 45 home runs at his longest
distance, what would the total distance be? _____

11. Player B's longest home run distance is 500 ft.
There are 5,280 ft in 1 mi. How many home
runs would Player B need to hit at his longest
distance for the total to be greater than 1 mi? _____

12. Which equation shows how you can find the number of
minutes in one year?

A $60 \times 24 \times 365$
B $60 \times 60 \times 24$
C 60×365
D $60 \times 60 \times 365$

13. Write a real-world problem where you would have to multiply 120 and 75.

_____

P 3·8

Problem Solving: Draw a Picture and Write an Equation

A hardware store ordered 9 packs of screws from a supplier. Each pack contains 150 screws. How many screws did the store order?

Read and Understand

What do you know?

The store ordered nine packs of screws.

Each pack contained 150 screws.

What are you trying to find?

The total number of screws ordered

Plan and Solve

Draw a picture of what you know.

screws 150	screws 150	
screws 150	screws 150	screws 150
screws 150	screws 150	screws 150

Write an equation.

Let x = the total number of screws.

$9 \times 150 = x$

Multiply.

$$\begin{array}{r} 4 \\ 150 \\ \times\ 9 \\ \hline 1{,}350 \end{array}$$

The store ordered 1,350 screws.

Look Back and Check

Is your answer reasonable?

Yes, $150 \times 10 = 1{,}500$.

A state aquarium has display tanks that each contains 75 fish. Three of these tanks are at the entrance. How many fish are on display at the entrance?

Draw a picture. Write an equation. Solve.

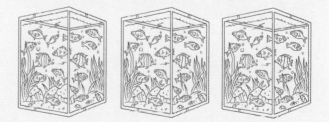

_____

Problem Solving: Draw a Picture and Write an Equation

Draw a picture and write an equation. Then solve.

1. When Mary was born, she weighed 8 pounds. When she was 10 years old, she weighed 10 times as much. How much did she weigh when she was 10 years old?

   _____

2. Sandi is 13 years old. Karla is 3 times Sandi's age. How old is Karla?

   _____

3. Hwong can fit 12 packets of coffee in a small box and 50 packets of coffee in a large box. Hwong has 10 small boxes and would like to reorganize them into large boxes. Which boxes should he use? Explain.

   _____

   _____

4. Daniel has 12 tennis balls. Manuel has twice as many tennis balls as Daniel. Kendra has twice as many balls as Manuel. How many tennis balls do they have in all?

   A 24   **B** 36   **C** 84   **D** 96

5. William travels only on Saturdays and Sundays and has flown 400 miles this month. Jason travels every weekday and has flown 500 miles this month. Who travels more miles *per day* for this month? Explain.

   _____

   _____

Dividing Multiples of 10 and 100

You can use math facts and patterns to help you divide mentally.

What is 480 ÷ 6?	What is 60,000 ÷ 6?
You already know that 48 ÷ 6 = 8.	60 ÷ 6 = 10
480 has one more zero than 48, so place one more zero in the quotient.	60,000 has three more zeros than 60, so place three zeros in the quotient.
48<u>0</u> ÷ 6 = 8<u>0</u>.	60,<u>000</u> ÷ 6 = 10,<u>000</u>.

Find each quotient. Use mental math.

1. 32 ÷ 8 = _____

2. 320 ÷ 8 = _____

3. 3,200 ÷ 8 = _____

4. 32,000 ÷ 8 = _____

5. 56 ÷ 7 = _____

6. 560 ÷ 7 = _____

7. 5,600 ÷ 7 = _____

8. 56,000 ÷ 7 = _____

9. 15 ÷ 3 = _____

10. 150 ÷ 3 = _____

11. 1,500 ÷ 3 = _____

12. 15,000 ÷ 3 = _____

13. Writing To Explain Explain how dividing 720 by 9 is like dividing 72 by 9.

_____

_____

Arlo has a newspaper delivery job. He wants to wrap each of his newspapers in a plastic bag to protect them from the rain. The newspapers are in bundles.

Arlo's Newspaper Delivery	
Number of bundles	12
Number of newspapers per bundle	9

Use mental math to answer the following questions.

14. How many bags will he use for 5 bundles? _____

15. How many bags will he use for 7 bundles? _____

16. How many bags will he use for all 12 bundles? _____

Name _____

Dividing Multiples of 10 and 100

Use mental math to find each quotient.

1. $27 \div 9 =$

2. $270 \div 9 =$

3. $2,700 \div 9 =$

_____   _____   _____

4. $24 \div 4 =$

5. $240 \div 4 =$

6. $2,400 \div 4 =$

_____   _____   _____

7. $720 \div 9 =$

8. $140 \div 7 =$

9. $2,100 \div 3 =$

_____   _____   _____

10. If a bike race covers 120 mi over 6 days and the cyclists ride the same distance each day, how many miles does each cyclist ride each day? _____

Use mental math to answer the following questions.

11. If the vehicles are divided evenly between the sections, how many vehicles are in each section?

Dealership Vehicle Storage
Sections of vehicles 4
Vehicles for sale 1,200
Rows per section 10

_____

12. If the vehicles are divided evenly between the rows in each section, how many vehicles are in each row?

_____

13. If $160,000 \div n = 4$, find n. _____

14. Find $32,000 \div 8$ mentally.

    A 4,000   **B** 400   **C** 40   **D** 4

15. Solve the equation $n \times 50 = 5,000$. Explain your solution.

_____

Estimating Quotients

There are several ways to adjust whole numbers to estimate quotients.

Example:

There are 216 students. The school has 8 classrooms. How many students will be in each classroom?

Estimate 216 ÷ 8.

Rounding	**Compatible Numbers**	**Multiplication**
You can use rounding to estimate a quotient.	You can use compatible numbers to estimate a quotient.	You can use multiplication to estimate a quotient.
Round 216 to the nearest hundred.	Change 216 to a compatible number for 8.	Think: 8 times what number is about 216?
In this case, 216 rounds to 200.	Compatible numbers for 8 are numbers divisible by 8, such as 160, 240, and 320. Choose 240, because it is the closest compatible number to 216.	$8 \times 25 = 200$
$200 \div 8 = 25$		$8 \times 30 = 240$
25 students per room is an underestimate, because 216 was rounded down to 200.	$240 \div 8 = 30$	216 is between 200 and 240. So a good estimate is a little more than 25 and a little less than 30 students per classroom.
	30 students per class is an overestimate, because 216 was rounded up to 240.	

Estimate each quotient. You may use any method.

1. 411 ÷ 2

2. 162 ÷ 4

_____

_____

3. Estimation If you estimate 342 ÷ 7 by using 350 ÷ 7 = 50, is 50 greater than or less than the exact answer? How did you decide? Is 50 an overestimate or an underestimate?

_____

_____

Estimating Quotients

Estimate each quotient. Tell which method you used.

1. $195 \div 4$ _____ _____

2. $283 \div 5$ _____ _____

3. $766 \div 8$ _____ _____

4. $179 \div 2$ _____ _____

5. $\$395.20 \div 5$ _____ _____

6. $\$31.75 \div 8$ _____ _____

7. $\$247.80 \div 5$ _____ _____

8. If you use $\$63.00 \div 9$ to estimate $\$62.59 \div 9$, is $7.00 greater than or less than the exact answer? Explain.

_____

_____

9. A band played 3 concerts and earned a total of $321.00. The band earned about the same amount for each concert. Estimate how much the band earned each night.

_____

_____

10. At a department store, a woman's total was $284.00 for 7 items. Estimate the average cost per item.

_____

11. Which is the closest estimate for $213 \div 4$?

   A 50   **B** 40   **C** 30   **D** 20

12. Explain how to estimate $524 \div 9$.

_____

_____

Problem Solving:
Reasonableness

After you solve a problem, check to see if your answer is reasonable.
Also check that you answered the right question.

Example:
74 students are going to a special class dinner where they will be
seated 8 to a table. Will 9 tables be enough?

Reasonableness
$74 \div 8 = 9$ R2

The answer is close to 9 tables.

Answering the right question

All students must have seats, so there must be
one more table to hold the remaining 2 students,
making 10 tables in all.

Tell whether each answer is reasonable.

1. Kendra wants to paste 500 photographs into an album, 6 photos
   to a page. She figures that she will need about 100 pages.

   _____

   _____

   _____

   _____

2. Hwong has 39 muffins. If each of his guests will eat 2 muffins,
   Hwong figures that he can serve muffins to 19 guests.

   _____

   _____

3. Ivan has a piece of lumber 104 inches long. He is sawing it
   into 12-inch lengths to make fence posts. He says he can get
   about 9 fence posts out of the board.

   _____

   _____

   _____

Name _____

Problem Solving: Reasonableness

Solve.

1. One tray holds eight sandwiches. If there are 30 sandwiches in all, how many trays are needed?

_____

2. There are 53 students on a field trip. One chaperone is needed for every 6 students. How many chaperones are needed?

_____

Mrs. Favicchio has 72 students in her science class. The table shows how many students can use each item of lab supplies she is ordering.

3. How many packets of pH paper does she need to order?

_____

4. How many cases of test tubes does she need to order?

_____

Lab Supplies	
Item	**Number of Students**
Packet of pH paper	10
Case of test tubes	5
Case of petri dishes	4

5. A loaf of banana bread serves 6 guests. There will be 47 guests attending the faculty breakfast. Which expression shows how many loaves are needed to serve them all?

  A 47 divided by 6 is 7 R 5, so 7 loaves are needed.

  B 47 divided by 6 is 7 R 5, so 8 loaves are needed.

  C 47 plus 6 is 53, so 53 loaves are needed.

  D 47 minus 6 is 41, so 41 loaves are needed.

6. **Writing To Explain** You are in line at an amusement park. You count 34 people in front of you. Each rollercoaster fits 11 people. How many rollercoasters must run before you can get on? Explain.

_____

_____

Connecting Models and Symbols

Divide 138 equally into
3 groups.

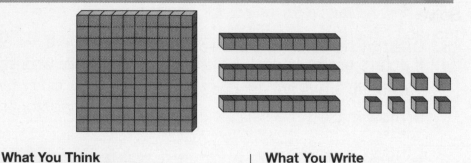

Step 1:

You can model 138 as
13 groups of 10 plus
8 ones.
Each group will get
4 groups of 10.
$40 \times 3 = 120$
$130 - 120 = 10$, so there
is 1 group of 10 left.

What You Think

What You Write

$$
\begin{array}{r}
4 \\
3\overline{)138} \\
-12 \\
\hline
1
\end{array}
$$

Step 2:

There is 1 group of 10 plus
1 group of 8 ones left. You
can model 18 as 18 ones.
$18 \div 3 = 6$, so each group
will also get 6 ones. There is
nothing left.

What You Think

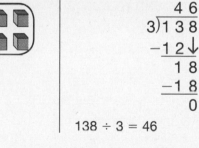

What You Write

$$
\begin{array}{r}
46 \\
3\overline{)138} \\
-12\downarrow \\
\hline
18 \\
-18 \\
\hline
0
\end{array}
$$

$138 \div 3 = 46$

Use models to help you divide.

1. $4\overline{)76}$

2. $2\overline{)94}$

3. $5\overline{)130}$

4. $7\overline{)238}$

5. $6\overline{)426}$

6. $3\overline{)264}$

7. If $n \div 3 = 57$, what is the value of n?

Name _____

Connecting Models and Symbols

After mowing lawns for one week, John put the money he earned on the table. There were four $100 bills, three $10 bills, and five $1 bills.

1. If John's brother borrowed one of the $100 bills and replaced it with ten $10 bills,

    a. how many $100 bills would there be? _____

    b. how many $10 bills would there be? _____

2. If John needed to divide the money evenly with two other workers, how much would each person receive? _____

3. If John needed to divide the money evenly with four other workers, how much would each person receive? _____

Complete each division problem. You may use play money or draw diagrams to help.

4.

$$4\,\overline{)1\ 3\ 6}$$

5.

$$3\,\overline{)1\ 6\ 2}$$

6. If $644.00 is divided equally among 7 people, how much will each person receive?

    A $82.00   B $92.00   C $93.00   D $103.00

7. **Writing To Explain** Write a story problem using two $100 bills, nine $10 bills, and seven $1 bills.

_____

_____

_____

Dividing by 1-Digit Divisors

Find 362 ÷ 5.

Step 1: To decide where to place the first digit in the quotient, compare the first digit of the dividend with the divisor.	Step 2: Divide the tens. Use multiplication facts and compatible numbers.	Step 3: Divide the ones. Use multiplication facts and compatible numbers.	Step 4: Check by multiplying.
3 < 5, so the first digit in the quotient will not go in the hundreds place.	Think 5 × ? = 35.	Think 5 × ? = 10	$5 \times 72 = 360$ $360 + 2 = 362$
Now, compare the first two digits of the dividend with the divisor.	Write 7 in the tens place of the quotient. Multiply. $5 \times 7 = 35$	Write 2 in the ones place of the quotient. Multiply. $5 \times 2 = 10$	
	$$\begin{array}{r} 7 \\ 5\overline{)3\ 6} \\ -3\ 5 \\ \hline 1 \end{array}$$	$$\begin{array}{r} 7\ 2\text{R}2 \\ 5\overline{)3\ 6\ 2} \\ -3\ 5\downarrow \\ \hline 1\ 2 \\ -1\ 0 \\ \hline 2 \end{array}$$	
36 > 5, so the first digit in the quotient will go in the tens place.	Subtract. 36 − 35 = 1 Compare. 1 < 5 Bring down the ones.	Subtract. 12 − 10 = 2 Compare. 2 < 5 There are no more digits to bring down, so 2 is the remainder.	

Divide. Check by multiplying.

1. $8\overline{)955}$

2. $7\overline{)249}$

3. $5\overline{)365}$

4. $8\overline{)448}$

5. $2\overline{)499}$

6. $6\overline{)396}$

7. How can you tell before you divide 425 by 9 that the first digit of the quotient is in the tens place?

_____

Name _____

Dividing by 1-Digit Divisors

Find each quotient.

1. 2)586   **2.** 3)565   **3.** 5)718   **4.** 4)599

5. 5)642   **6.** 6)354   **7.** 9)210   **8.** 8)927

The Paez family lives in Louisville, Kentucky, and has decided to take a road trip for their summer vacation.

9. How many miles will the Paez family drive each day if they decide to take 5 days to drive 865 mi to Dallas? _____

10. The Paez family decides they want to drive 996 mi to Boston in 6 days. How many miles will they drive each day? _____

11. If a staff of 9 people had to clean a hotel with 198 rooms, how many rooms would each person have to clean if they divided the rooms equally?

  A 29   **B** 25   **C** 23   **D** 22

12. Explain how to check the quotient from a division problem.

_____

_____

_____

Name _____

Zeros in the Quotient

Find 816 ÷ 4.

Step 1: Compare the first digit of the dividend with the divisor. 8 > 4, so the first digit in the quotient will go in the hundreds place.

Divide the hundreds. Think 4 × ? = 8.

Write 2 in the hundreds place of the quotient. Multiply. 4 × 2 = 8

$$\begin{array}{r} 2 \\ 4\overline{)8\ 1} \\ -8\downarrow \\ \hline 0\ 1 \end{array}$$

Subtract. 8 − 8 = 0

Compare. 0 < 4

Bring down the tens.

Step 2: Compare. 1 < 4

You cannot divide the tens, so place 0 in the tens place of the quotient.

Bring down the ones.

$$\begin{array}{r} 2\ 0 \\ 4\overline{)8\ 1\ 6} \\ -8\downarrow \\ \hline 0\ 1\ 6 \end{array}$$

Step 3: Compare. 16 > 4

Divide the ones. Think 4 × ? = 16.

Write 4 in the ones place of the quotient.

Multiply. 4 × 4 = 16

Subtract. 16 − 16 = 0

Compare. 0 < 4

There are no more digits to bring down, so the problem is done.

$$\begin{array}{r} 2\ 0\ 4 \\ 4\overline{)8\ 1\ 6} \\ -8 \\ \hline 0\ 1\ 6 \\ -\ 1\ 6 \\ \hline 0 \end{array}$$

Step 4: Check by multiplying.
4 × 204 = 816

Find each quotient. Check your answers by multiplying.

1. 8)640

2. 3)322

3. 4)908

4. 15)225

5. 6)624

6. 6)965

7. Is 593 ÷ 6 a little less than 10, a little more than 10, a little less than 100, or a little more than 100? Explain.

_____

_____

Name _____

Zeros in the Quotient

Find each quotient. Check your answers by multiplying.

1. $490 \div 7 =$ _____   **2.** $326 \div 3 =$ _____

3. $916 \div 3 =$ _____   **4.** $720 \div 2 =$ _____

5. $2\overline{)941}$ **6.** $9\overline{)982}$ **7.** $7\overline{)740}$ **8.** $5\overline{)703}$

9. If there are 505 seats in an auditorium divided equally into 5 sections, how many seats are in each section?

_____

10. A book company publishes 749 copies of a novel and distributes them to 7 bookstores. If each bookstore were to receive the same number of copies, how many copies would be sent to each store?

_____

11. In one year, Dolores and Tom's four children saved $420 by recycling cans. When they divided the money equally, how much money did each child receive?

A $50   **B** $100   **C** $105   **D** $1,500

12. Writing To Explain Explain why estimating before you divide $624 \div 6$ helps you place the first digit in the quotient.

_____

_____

_____

Problem Solving: Draw a Picture and Write an Equation

Mr. Rodriguez needs to store 10 test tubes in racks that hold 4 test tubes apiece. How many racks does he need?

Draw a picture.

10 test tubes

? racks

4

test tubes per rack

Write an equation.

Let r be the number of test-tube racks needed.

$$10 \div 4 = r$$

Solve the problem.

$$r = 2 \text{ R } 2$$

Think: R 2 means that 2 test tubes are still left. Since they must be in a rack, one more rack is needed.

Write the answer in a complete sentence.

Mr. Rodriguez will need three test-tube racks.

Mr. Rodriguez could also use racks that hold three test tubes or racks that hold five test tubes. Which racks should he use if he wants each rack completely filled? Explain.

_____

_____

Name _____

Problem Solving: Draw a Picture and Write an Equation

Draw a picture and write an equation. Then solve.

1. Tommy paid $39 to fill up the gas tank in his car. If one gallon of gas costs $3, how many gallons of gas did Tommy put in?

   _____

   _____

2. To prepare for the brunch, Ivana needs to place 8 muffins in each basket. If she has 115 muffins, how many baskets will she need?

   _____

   _____

3. Write a real-world problem that you can solve by writing an equation. The answer to the problem must be 6.

   _____

   _____

4. The perimeter is the distance around an object. The perimeter of a square is 84 centimeters. What is the length of one side of the square?

   A 75 cm   **B** 42 cm   **C** 21 cm   **D** 14 cm

5. **Writing to Explain** A perfect score on a quiz is 100. Mrs. Frisoli gives students 1 point for putting their name on the paper. If there are only 9 questions on the quiz, how much is each question worth? Explain how you found your answer.

   _____

   _____

Name _____

Using Patterns to Divide

You can use basic facts and patterns to divide mentally.

Using basic facts	Using patterns
What is 350 ÷ 70?	What is 5,400 ÷ 60?
Think: 350 ÷ 70 is the same as 35 tens ÷ 7 tens.	5,400 ÷ 60 is the same as 540 ÷ 6.
35 ÷ 7 = 5	54 ÷ 6 = 9, so 540 ÷ 6 = 90.
So, 350 ÷ 70 = 5.	So, 5,400 ÷ 60 = 90.

Find each quotient. Use mental math.

1. 280 ÷ 70 = _____

2. 320 ÷ 40 = _____

3. 360 ÷ 60 = _____

4. 7,200 ÷ 80 = _____

5. 9,000 ÷ 30 = _____

6. 4,800 ÷ 80 = _____

7. 2,000 ÷ 40 = _____

8. 5,600 ÷ 70 = _____

9. How is dividing 250 by 50 the same as dividing 2,500 by 500?

_____

_____

_____

10. Explain how you can mentally determine that 35,000 ÷ 70 = 500.

_____

_____

_____

Name _____

Using Patterns to Divide

In **1** through **4**, find each quotient. Use mental math.

1. 360 ÷ 40 = 36 tens ÷ 4 tens = _____

2. 5,400 ÷ 90 = 540 tens ÷ 9 tens = _____

3. 240 ÷ 30 = 24 tens ÷ 3 tens = _____

4. 4,800 ÷ 10 = 480 tens ÷ 1 ten = _____

Use mental math to answer the following questions.

5. If the vehicles are divided evenly
   among the sections, how many
   vehicles are in each section?

   _____

Dealership Vehicle Storage	
Sections of vehicles	4
Vehicles for sale	1,200
Rows per section	10

6. If the vehicles are divided evenly among the rows
   in each section, how many vehicles are in each row?

   _____

7. Suppose there are 297 students going on a field trip. If each
   schoolbus can carry 58 students, estimate the number of
   buses that will be needed to transport all the students.

   _____

   _____

8. If $1,600 ÷ n = 4$, what is the value of n?

   A 40   **B** 400   **C** 4,000   **D** 40,000

9. Solve the equation $n × 50 = 5,000$. Explain your solution.

   _____

   _____

Name _____

Estimating Quotients with 2-Digit Divisors

You can use compatible numbers to estimate a quotient.

Find 175 ÷ 32.

Step 1: Find compatible numbers for 175 and 32.

32 rounds to 30.

Think: 18 can be divided evenly by 3.

180 is close to 175 and 30 is close to 32.

180 and 30 are compatible numbers.

Step 2: Divide. Use patterns to help you, if possible.

Think: 180 ÷ 30 is the same as 18 tens ÷ 3 tens.

18 ÷ 3 = 6
So, 180 ÷ 30 = 6.

Step 3: Check for reasonableness.

6 × 30 = 180

So, a good estimate of 175 ÷ 32 is 6.

Estimate each quotient using compatible numbers.

1. 298 ÷ 25 _____

2. 5,391 ÷ 77 _____

3. 24,303 ÷ 12 _____

4. 276 ÷ 42 _____

5. 1,347 ÷ 54 _____

6. 5,564 ÷ 91 _____

At Elmer Elementary School, fifth-grade students are saving money for a summer trip to Washington, D.C.

7. The money Percy has saved is how many times as great as the money James has saved?

_____

_____

Student	Amount Saved
Percy	$125
Emily	$ 80
George	$202
James	$ 41
Bertha	$159

R 5·2

Estimating Quotients with 2-Digit Divisors

In **1** through **4**, estimate the quotients using compatible numbers.

1. $566 \div 81 =$ _____

2. $453 \div 93 =$ _____

3. $1,423 \div 69 =$ _____

4. $8,631 \div 10 =$ _____

5. If you use $\$99.00 \div 11$ to estimate $\$98.69 \div 11$, is $\$9.00$ greater than or less than the exact answer? Explain.

_____

_____

6. Suppose there are 19 students in a class. A teacher has 122 pencils and passes them out to the class. Estimate the number of pencils each student will receive. _____

7. At a department store, a package of 12 handkerchiefs costs $\$58.99$. Estimate how much each handkerchief costs. _____

8. Which is the closest estimate for $2,130 \div 33$?

A 7   **B** 17   **C** 70   **D** 700

9. Explain how to estimate $498 \div 12$.

_____

_____

Connecting Models and Symbols

Divide 345 by 15.

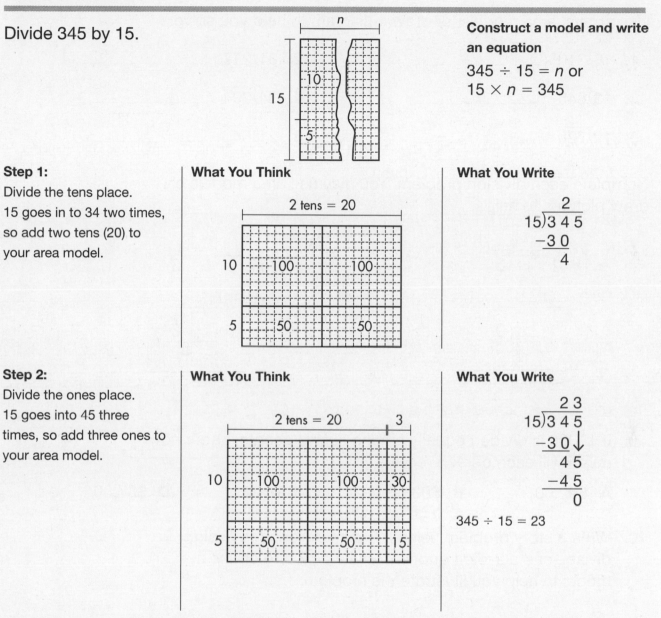

Construct a model and write an equation

$345 \div 15 = n$ or
$15 \times n = 345$

Step 1:

Divide the tens place.
15 goes in to 34 two times,
so add two tens (20) to
your area model.

What You Think

2 tens = 20

10   100   100
5   50   50

What You Write

$$\begin{array}{r} 2 \\ 15\overline{)345} \\ -3\,0 \\ \hline 4 \end{array}$$

Step 2:

Divide the ones place.
15 goes into 45 three
times, so add three ones to
your area model.

What You Think

2 tens = 20   3

10   100   100   30
5   50   50   15

What You Write

$$\begin{array}{r} 2\,3 \\ 15\overline{)345} \\ -3\,0\downarrow \\ \hline 4\,5 \\ -4\,5 \\ \hline 0 \end{array}$$

$345 \div 15 = 23$

Use models to help you divide.

1. $12\overline{)228}$

2. $20\overline{)940}$

3. $15\overline{)390}$

Name _____

Connecting Models and Symbols

Use arrays, area models, or draw a diagram to help you solve.

1. $10\overline{)210}$ _____

2. $31\overline{)217}$ _____

3. $13\overline{)845}$ _____

4. $34\overline{)204}$ _____

5. $12\overline{)720}$ _____

6. $21\overline{)640}$ _____

Complete each division problem. You may use area models or draw pictures to help.

7.

$14\overline{)2\ 1\ 0}$

8.

$19\overline{)2\ 2\ 8}$

9. If $1000 is divided equally among twelve people, about how much will each person receive?

A $92.00   **B** $83.00   **C** $91.00   **D** $87.00

10. Write a story problem using a 3-digit dividend, a 2-digit divisor, and a 2-digit quotient. Draw a picture or use a model to help you illustrate the problem.

_____

_____

_____

_____

Dividing by Multiples of 10

Find 623 ÷ 40.

Step 1: Estimate the quotient using compatible numbers, $600 ÷ 40 = 15$. Then, divide the tens.

```
     1
40)623    Divide 62 ÷ 40
  -40     Multiply 1 × 40 = 40
   22     Subtract 62 - 40 = 22
          Compare 22 < 40
```

Step 2: Bring down the ones. Then, divide the ones.

```
     15
40)623
  -40↓
   223    Divide 223 ÷ 40
  -200    Multiply 5 × 40 = 200
    23    Subtract 223 - 200 = 23
```

Step 3: Since 23 < 40, write 23 as the remainder in the quotient.

```
    15 R23
40)623
  -40↓
   223
  -200
    23    Compare 23 < 40
```

Complete.

1. 60)288

2. 20)455

3. 80)866

4. 30)233

5. 50)498

6. Celia plans to pack her books in boxes when her family moves. Each box will hold 20 books. Celia has 97 books. How many boxes will she need to pack all her books?

_____

Name _____

Dividing by Multiples of 10

In **1** through **6**, divide.

1. 20)̄467   _____   **2.** 40)̄321   _____

3. 80)̄813   _____   **4.** 40)̄284   _____

5. 90)̄648   _____   **6.** 10)̄587   _____

7. To drive from New York City, NY, to
Los Angeles, CA, you must drive about
2,779 miles. If you drive 60 miles per
hour , about how many hours
would you spend driving?   _____

8. Suppose one bottle of paint can cover 20 tiles. You have
348 tiles. How many bottles of paint do you need to buy
to cover all 348 tiles? Explain.

_____

_____

9. A group of 483 students is taking a field trip. One bus is
needed for every 50 students. How many buses are needed?

_____

10. A decagon is a ten-sided figure. If a regular decagon has a
perimeter of 114 centimeters, how long is each side of the figure?

A 11.4 cm   **B** 14 cm   **C** 114 cm   **D** 124 cm

11. To figure out how many hours it will take to drive from his home to his cousin's
house, a student divides 289 by 60 and estimates that it will take about 4.5
hours. Explain whether you think this is a reasonable estimate.

_____

_____

1-Digit Quotients

Find $436 \div 53$.

To find the answer, first estimate the quotient.

Think: $400 \div 50 = 8$ or $450 \div 50 = 9$

Try 9:

```
        9
53)436
   -477
```

Write 9 in the ones place.
Multiply, $9 \times 53 = 477$.
$477 > 436$.
This estimate is too high.

Try 8:

```
        8
53)436
   -424
     12
```

Write 8 in the ones place.
Multiply, $8 \times 53 = 424$.
Subtract, $436 - 424 = 12$.
Compare, $12 < 53$. Write the remainder in the quotient.

$436 \div 53 = 8 \text{ R}12$
Check:
$8 \times 53 = 424$
$424 + 12 = 436$

Complete.

```
         7 R                          R12                          R
1. 32)245              2. 64)332                  3. 51)489
```

Divide. Check by multiplying.

4. 49)216   **5.** 79)698   **6.** 25)194

7. Explain how you know the answer to the problem below
   has an error.

```
      2 R86         _____
77)240
   -154            _____
     86
```

Name _____

1-Digit Quotients

In **1** through **6**, find each quotient.

1. 37)‾120‾

2. 39)‾342‾

3. 62)‾338‾

4. 42)‾284‾

5. 82)‾599‾

6. 55)‾474‾

7. Solomon has $118. He wants to purchase concert tickets for himself and 5 friends. Each ticket costs $19. Does he have enough money? Explain.

_____

_____

8. Which problem will have the greater quotient, 376.0 ÷ 93 OR 376 ÷ 93.01? Explain how you know.

_____

_____

_____

9. Which is 458 ÷ 73?

A 5 R19   **B** 5 R20   **C** 6 R19   **D** 6 R20

10. A student solves the problem 354 ÷ 24. The student finds an answer of 13 R40. Explain how you can tell that the answer is incorrect just by looking at the remainder.

_____

_____

_____

2-Digit Quotients

Find 866 ÷ 34.

Step 1: Round the divisor to the nearest ten. Look at the first digit in the divisor and the first digit in the dividend. What basic division fact is the best estimate of the quotient of these two numbers?

$$34\overline{)866} \quad\longrightarrow\quad 30\overline{)866}$$

$$8 \div 3 = 2\ \text{R}2$$

Step 2: Use this fact to begin the quotient. Write it over the tens place.

$$\begin{array}{r} 2 \\ 34\overline{)866} \\ -68\downarrow \\ \hline 186 \end{array}$$

Multiply, $2 \times 34 = 68$. Subtract and bring down the next digit in the dividend.

Step 3: What basic division fact is the best estimate of the next division? Use this fact and write it over the ones place.

$$\begin{array}{r} 25\ \text{R}16 \\ 34\overline{)866} \\ -68 \\ \hline 186 \\ -170 \\ \hline 16 \end{array}$$

Multiply, $5 \times 34 = 170$. Subtract. Compare the remainder with the divisor. If the remainder is less than the divisor, write it in the quotient.

Check.
$25 \times 34 = 850$
$850 + 16 = 866$

Complete.

1. $\begin{array}{r} 11\ \text{R}\ \square \\ 39\overline{)437} \end{array}$

2. $\begin{array}{r} \square\square\ \text{R}3 \\ 24\overline{)627} \end{array}$

3. $\begin{array}{r} \square\square\ \text{R}\square \\ 26\overline{)917} \end{array}$

Divide. Check by multiplying.

4. $13\overline{)175}$

5. $44\overline{)508}$

6. April has 95 baseball cards. She wants to organize them on pages that hold 18 cards each. She has 5 pages. Does April have enough pages to organize all her cards?

Name _____

2-Digit Quotients

In **1** through **6**, find each quotient.

1. 14)‾413‾   _____

2. 29)‾634‾   _____

3. 35)‾768‾   _____

4. 19)‾401‾   _____

5. 45)‾942‾   _____

6. 26)‾503‾   _____

7. The school student council sponsored a Switch Day where students were able to switch classes every 20 minutes. The students are in school for 7 hours. If a student switched as often as possible, how many classrooms in all did that student visit? (Hint: There are 60 minutes in 1 hour.)

_____

8. 456 students participated in Switch Day. The students raised money for charity so that the principal would approve of the day. If the total amount of money raised was $912, and each student brought in the same amount of money, how much did each student raise?

_____

9. The total dinner bill at a buffet came out to $589 for 31 people. About how much was the buffet cost per person?

   A $15.00   **B** $20.00   **C** $22.00   **D** $25.00

10. If you have a two-digit divisor and a three-digit dividend, does the quotient always have the same number of digits?

_____

_____

Estimating and Dividing with Greater Numbers

Find 8,037 ÷ 77.

You can use a calculator to divide large numbers.

Step 1: Estimate. Round the divisor and the dividend.

8,037 ÷ 77 ⟶
8,000 ÷ 80 = 100

The quotient should be close to 100.

Step 2: Now, use a calculator to find the quotient.

8,037 ÷ 77

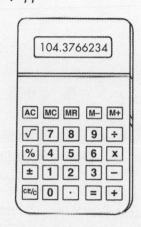

104.3766234

Step 3: Round the quotient to the required place. Remember, if the digit is 5 or more, add 1 to the rounding digit. If the digit is less than 5, leave the rounding digit alone.

Round the quotient to the nearest hundredth. 104.3766234 rounded to the nearest hundredth is 104.38. This is close to the original estimate, so the answer is reasonable.

Estimate first. Then use a calculator to find the quotient. Round to the nearest hundredth if necessary.

1. 78)3,796

2. 51)2,588

3. 38)3,914

4. 37)7,492

5. 46)6,725

6. 62)9,911

7. Is 5,309 ÷ 26 less than 20, greater than 20 but less than 200, or greater than 200?

Estimating and Dividing with Greater Numbers

Estimate first. Then use a calculator to find the quotient. Round to the nearest hundredth if necessary.

1. $53\overline{)6{,}324}$ **2.** $52\overline{)6{,}348}$ **3.** $86\overline{)31{,}309}$ **4.** $33\overline{)3{,}455}$

5. $17{,}496 \div 91 =$ _____   **6.** $25{,}214 \div 47 =$ _____

7. $2{,}312 \div 26 =$ _____   **8.** $4{,}895 \div 83 =$ _____

The Humphrey family decided to fly from San Francisco to New York City, and from there to Rome, New Delhi, and finally Tokyo.

9. It took the Humphrey family 6 hours to travel from San Francisco to New York. How many kilometers did they travel per hour?

Distances by Plane	
San Francisco to New York	4,140 km
New York to Rome	6,907 km
Rome to New Delhi	5,929 km
New Delhi to Tokyo	5,857 km

_____

10. During the flight from New Delhi to Tokyo, flight attendants came through with snacks every 600 km. How many times did they come through?

_____

11. When the family arrived in New Delhi from Rome, the youngest son asked the pilot how fast he was flying the plane. The pilot told him about 847 km per hour. How many hours did it take the family to fly from Rome to New Delhi?

A 5 h   **B** 6 h   **C** 7 h   **D** 8 h

12. Write a word problem that would require you to use $5{,}621 \div 23$.

_____

Problem Solving: Missing or Extra Information

Aiko bought 6 red balloons and 11 clear balloons for a party. During the party, 3 clear balloons burst but none of the red balloons did. How many clear balloons did Aiko have after the party?

Read and Understand

What do you know?

Aiko bought 6 red balloons.

Aiko bought 11 clear balloons.

Three clear balloons burst during the party.

No red balloons burst during the party.

What are you trying to find?

The number of clear balloons remaining after the party

Plan and Solve

Draw a picture of what you know.

Solve the problem.

$11 - 3 = 8$

Write the answer in a complete sentence.

Aiko had 8 clear balloons after the party.

Look Back and Check

Is your answer correct?

Yes, $8 + 3 = 11$

Look back at the items listed in "What you know."

1. What information helped you solve the problem?

_____

2. What information did **NOT** help you solve the problem?

_____

Name _____

Problem Solving: Missing or Extra Information

Decide if each problem has extra or missing information.
Solve if possible.

1. It takes 4 hours to drive from Boston to New York. Jordan
has a meeting in New York at 2:00 P.M. Can she arrive at her
meeting on time?

_____

2. Franco hikes 4 miles each day for 5 days. He carries
100 ounces of water with him. It takes him 1 hour to hike
4 miles. How many hours did he hike in 5 days?

_____

3. Write a real-world problem that gives extra information.
Under the problem write what the extra information is.

_____

4. Jorge buys T-shirts for $4 each and paints designs on them.
He sells the designed T-shirts for $7 each. What information
is needed to find how much profit he makes in one week?

    A The price of T-shirts at a store

    B The color of the T-shirts that he buys

    C The types of designs he draws on the T-shirts

    D The number of T-shirts he sells in one week

5. Krista can type 60 words per minute. She wrote an essay
by hand in 5 hours, and it is now 4 pages long and has 500
words in it. She wants to type up her essay. About how long
will it take to type her essay? Write what the extra or missing
information is. Then solve if possible.

_____

Multiplying Decimals by 10, 100, or 1,000

You can use patterns to multiply decimals mentally by 10, 100, and 1,000.

Andrew starts selling his baseball cards for $0.10 each. After selling 10 cards, he has made $1.00. After selling 100 cards, he has made $10.00.

$.0.10 $.0.10 × 10 = $1.00 $0.10 × 100 = $10.00

When you multiply by

10 (10^1)	Add 1 zero
100 (10^2)	Add 2 zeros
1,000 (10^3)	Add 3 zeros

If Andrew sold 1,000 cards, how much money would he make? _____

Mental Math For questions **1** through **4**, find the product using mental math.

1. 6.1×10 _____

2. 100×37.98 _____

3. $92.3 \times 1,000$ _____

4. 0.418×100 _____

5. Myla has an antique flower vase that she bought for $15.75 many years ago. The vase's value is now 1,000 times as great. What is the value of the vase? _____

6. Raul can hit a golf ball 26.4 yards. A.J. can hit a golf ball 10 times as far. How far can A.J. hit the ball? _____

7. Is 0.018 a reasonable answer for 1.8×100?

_____

_____

Name _____

Multiplying Decimals by 10, 100, or 1,000

Use mental math to find each product.

1. 53.7 × 10 _____

2. 74.3 × 100 _____

3. 66.37 × 1,000 _____

4. 1.03 × 10 _____

5. 92.5 × 10 _____

6. 0.8352 × 100 _____

7. 0.567 × 100 _____

8. 572.6 × 1,000 _____

9. 5.8 × 100 _____

10. 0.21 × 1,000 _____

11. 6.2 × 1,000 _____

12. 1.02 × 10 _____

13. 0.003 × 1,000 _____

14. 0.002 × 10 _____

15. 7.03 × 10 _____

16. 4.06 × 100 _____

17. Kendra bought 10 gallons of gasoline at $3.26 per gallon. How much did she pay for the gasoline?

    A $326.00   **B** $32.60   **C** $1.26   **D** $0.26

18. Freddy is helping buy ingredients for salads for the school spaghetti dinner. He bought 10 pounds of onions at $0.69 per pound, 100 pounds of tomatoes at $0.99 pound, 1,000 pounds of bread crumbs at $0.09 per pound, and 100 pounds of lettuce at $0.69 per pound. Which of the items he bought cost the most?

    A tomatoes   **B** lettuce   **C** bread crumbs   **D** onions

19. Marco and Suzi each multiplied 0.721 × 100. Marco got 7.21 for his product. Suzi got 72.1 for her product. Which student multiplied correctly? How do you know?

_____

_____

Name _____

Estimating the Product of a Decimal and a Whole Number

You can estimate when you are multiplying a decimal by a whole number to check the reasonableness of your product.

Zane needs to buy 27 lb of roast beef for the company party. The roast beef costs $2.98 per pound. About how much will the roast beef cost?

There are two ways to estimate.

Round both numbers

$2.98 × 27
 ↓   ↓
 $3 × 30 = $90

The roast beef will cost about $90.

Adjust your factors to compatible numbers you can multiply mentally.

$2.98 × 27
 ↓   ↓
 $3 × 25 = $75

The roast beef will cost about $75.

Estimate each product.

1. 0.8 × 22 _____

2. 19.3 × 6 _____

3. 345 × 5.79 _____

4. 966 × 0.46 _____

Use the chart to answer questions 5 through 7.

5. About how much would it cost for Angelina and her 4 sisters to get a shampoo and a haircut?

_____

_____

Treatment	Cost
Shampoo	$7.95
Haircut	$12.95
Coloring	$18.25
Perm	$22.45

6. Could 3 of the sisters get their hair colored for less than $100?

_____

7. Angelina gets 9 haircuts per year. About how much does she spend on haircuts for the year?

_____

 R 6·2

Name _____

Estimating the Product of a Decimal and a Whole Number

Estimate each product using rounding or compatible numbers.

1. 0.97 × 312

_____

2. 8.02 × 70

_____

3. 31.04 × 300

_____

4. 0.56 × 48

_____

5. 0.33 × 104

_____

6. 0.83 × 12

_____

7. 0.89 × 51

_____

8. 4.05 × 11

_____

9. 0.13 × 7

_____

10. 45.1 × 5

_____

11. 99.3 × 92

_____

12. 47.2 × 93

_____

13. Mr. Webster works 4 days a week at his office and 1 day a week at home. The distance to Mr. Webster's office is 23.7 miles. He takes a different route home, which is 21.8 miles. When Mr. Webster works at home, he drives to the post office once a day, which is 2.3 miles from his house. Which piece of information is not important in figuring out how many miles Mr. Webster drives per week to his office?

    A the number of days at the office

    B the distance to his office

    C the distance to the post office

    D the distance from his office

14. Mrs. Smith bought her three children new snowsuits for winter. Each snowsuit cost $25.99. How much did Mrs. Smith pay in all?

    A $259.90   **B** $77.97   **C** $51.98   **D** $25.99

15. How can estimating be helpful before finding an actual product?

_____

_____

_____

Number Sense: Decimal Multiplication

Amelia can walk 3.6 miles in one hour. How far will she walk in 2.1 hours?

Step 1. Estimate	Step 2. Compare each factor to 1 to determine the relative size of the product.	Step 3. Multiply as you would with whole numbers. Use reasoning to place the decimal appropriately.
$3.5 \times 2 = 7$	$3.6 > 1$ $2.1 > 1$ Because both factors are greater than 1, your answer will be greater than both factors.	$\begin{array}{r} 3.6 \\ \times\ 2.1 \\ \hline 3\ 6 \\ 7\ 2\ 0 \\ \hline 7.5\ 6 \end{array}$ ↑

Amelia will walk 7.56 miles in 2.1 hours.

Solve. Check your answer for reasonableness.

1. $\begin{array}{r} 1.6 \\ \times\ 0.3 \\ \hline \end{array}$

2. $\begin{array}{r} 0.8 \\ \times\ 0.2 \\ \hline \end{array}$

3. $\begin{array}{r} 12.8 \\ \times\ 3.2 \\ \hline \end{array}$

4. $\begin{array}{r} 0.03 \\ \times\ 6 \\ \hline \end{array}$

5. Explain why $0.3 \times 0.9 \neq 2.7$. What is the correct answer?

_____

_____

6. **Mental Math** Estimate the product of 3.9 and 4.6 using mental math. Explain the method you used.

_____

_____

Number Sense: Decimal Multiplication

For 1-8 only two numbers of the product are shown. Also, the decimal point is missing. Complete the product and place the decimal point where it should be. Round your answer to the nearest hundredth.

1. $0.4 \times 0.6 =$ 2 4   **5.** $0.2 \times 0.8 =$ 1 6

2. $3.6 \times 4.1 =$ 1 4   **6.** $4.04 \times 3 =$ 1 2

3. $9.01 \times 8.3 =$ 7 4   **7.** $11.6 \times 3.4 =$ 3 9

4. $4.06 \times 20.1 =$ 8 1.   **8.** $7.8 \times 0.1 =$ 7 8

For 9-12 complete the operation and explain why you placed the decimal point where you did.

9. $1.8 \times 0.3 =$ _____

_____

10. $0.2 \times 0.7 =$ _____

_____

11. $12.4 \times 3.1 =$ _____

_____

12. $9.5 \times 3 =$ _____

_____

Models for Multiplying Decimals

Use the same strategy to multiply a decimal by a whole number
or to multiply a decimal by a decimal.

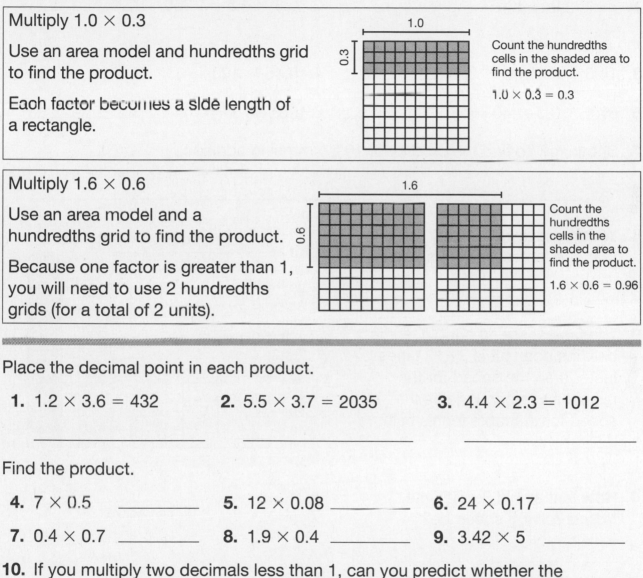

Multiply 1.0 × 0.3

Use an area model and hundredths grid
to find the product.

Each factor becomes a side length of
a rectangle.

Count the hundredths
cells in the shaded area to
find the product.

1.0 × 0.3 = 0.3

Multiply 1.6 × 0.6

Use an area model and a
hundredths grid to find the product.

Because one factor is greater than 1,
you will need to use 2 hundredths
grids (for a total of 2 units).

Count the
hundredths
cells in the
shaded area to
find the product.

1.6 × 0.6 = 0.96

Place the decimal point in each product.

1. 1.2 × 3.6 = 432   **2.** 5.5 × 3.7 = 2035   **3.** 4.4 × 2.3 = 1012

_____   _____   _____

Find the product.

4. 7 × 0.5 _____   **5.** 12 × 0.08 _____   **6.** 24 × 0.17 _____

7. 0.4 × 0.7 _____   **8.** 1.9 × 0.4 _____   **9.** 3.42 × 5 _____

10. If you multiply two decimals less than 1, can you predict whether the
product will be less than or greater than either of the factors? Explain.

_____

_____

Models for Multiplying Decimals

Place the decimal point in each product.

1. $3 \times 6.89 = 2067$ _____

2. $0.3 \times 4.5 = 1350$ _____

Find each product.

3. $14.3 \times 2.1 \times 8 =$ _____

4. $0.45 \times 100 =$ _____

5. $67.1 \times 0.3 \times 40 =$ _____

6. $58 \times 4.21 =$ _____

7. Show how to find the product of 16.2×4 using addition.

_____

8. Which activity is 6 times faster than the fastest rowing speed?

_____

9. The fastest speed a table tennis ball has been hit is 21.12 times faster than the speed for the fastest swimmer. What is the speed for the table tennis ball?

_____

10. How fast would 3 times the fastest rowing speed be?

_____

Fastest Sporting Speeds

11. Which is the product of 241.82×3.1?

A 7.498   **B** 749.642   **C** 74.958   **D** 7.5

12. Explain why multiplying 37.4×0.1 gives a product that is less than 37.4.

_____

_____

Multiplying a Decimal by a Whole Number

Travis can read a book chapter in 2.6 hours. The book has 18 chapters. How long will it take Travis to read the book?

Step 1. Use powers of 10 to multiply as you would with whole numbers.

$2.6 \times 10^1 = 26$
$18 \times 1 = 18$

$$\begin{array}{r} 26 \\ \times\ 18 \\ \hline 208 \\ +\ 260 \\ \hline 468 \end{array}$$

Step 2. Divide the whole number answer by 10^1 so that the number of decimal places in the factors and the product does not change.

$468 \div 10^1 = 46.8$

Step 3. Use reasoning to check your answer. Since 2.6 is greater than one, the answer should be greater than 18. Because 46.8 is greater than 18, your answer is reasonable.

It will take Travis 46.8 hours to read the book.

For questions **1** through **3**, find the product.

1. $\begin{array}{r} 2.3 \\ \times\ 6 \\ \hline \end{array}$

2. $\begin{array}{r} 71.7 \\ \times\ 12 \\ \hline \end{array}$

3. $\begin{array}{r} 0.89 \\ \times\ 21 \\ \hline \end{array}$

4. Sara is making pillows. Each pillow requires 1.7 yards of fabric. How many yards of fabric will Sara need to make 9 pillows?

_____

5. Light bulbs usually cost $2. They are on sale for 0.50 of the regular price. What is the sale price? Is this a better price than if the sale price were 0.35 of the regular price?

_____

_____

Name _____

Multiplying a Decimal by a Whole Number

Find each product.

1. 5.4	2. 3.8	3. 0.55	4. 8.19
× 3	× 4	× 8	× 5

Insert a decimal point in each answer to make the equation true.

5. $5 \times 6.3 = 315$ _____

6. $3.01 \times 9 = 2709$ _____

Use the table at the right for Exercises **7–9.**

7. Which desert accumulates the least amount of rain in August?

_____

8. If each month in Reno had the same average rainfall as in August, what would the total number of millimeters be after 12 months?

_____

Average Desert Rainfall in August

Desert	Average Rainfall
Reno	0.19 mm
Sahara	0.17 mm
Mojave	0.1 mm
Tempe	0.24 mm

9. In December, the average total rainfall in all of the deserts together is 0.89 mm. Explain how to use the figures from the table to write a comparison of the total desert rainfall in August and December.

_____

_____

_____

10. If $4n = 3.60$, which is the value of n?

A 0.09   **B** 0.9   **C** 9   **D** 90

Multiplying Two Decimals

Caroline earns $2.40 per hour for babysitting her brother. She babysat last night for 3.25 hours. How much did she earn?

First, estimate your product so you can check for reasonableness.

$2.40 × 3.25

↓   ↓

$2 × 3 = 6   Caroline earned about $6.00.

Step 1: Multiply each factor by powers of 10 to create whole numbers. Then multiply these numbers.

$2.40 × 10^2 = 240$
$3.25 × 10^2 = 325$

```
        325
    ×   240
        000
     13,000
    +65,000
     78,000
```

Step 2: Because you multipled each factor by 10^2, you must divide your answer by 10^2 two times.

$78,000 ÷ 10^4 = 7.8000$

$7.8000 = \$7.80$

Caroline earned $7.80 last night. Because $7.80 is close to your estimate of $6, your answer is reasonable.

Find each product. Check by estimating.

1. 0.2 × 4.6 _____

2. 3.9 × 7.1 _____

3. 8.54 × 0.1 _____

4. 0.53 × 6.4 _____

5. 9.3 × 5.86 _____

6. 0.37 × 4.4 _____

7. Jackie wants to buy a new CD player. It costs $32.95. She has saved $26 and has a coupon for 30% off the price. Does Jackie have enough money to buy the CD player?

_____

_____

_____

Name _____

Multiplying Two Decimals

Find each product.

1. 3.2
    $\times$ 0.3

2. 4.4
    $\times$ 0.2

3. 8.6
    $\times$ 3.4

4.   1.9
    $\times$ 0.05

5. 0.79 $\times$ 4.3 = _____

6. 0.8 $\times$ 0.05 = _____

7. The product of 4.7 and 6.5 equals 30.55. What is the product of 4.7 and 0.65? 4.7 and 65?

_____

8. What would be the gravity in relation to Earth of a planet with 3.4 times the gravity of Mercury?

_____

Relative (to Earth) Surface Gravity

Planet	Gravity
Mercury	0.39
Neptune	1.22
Jupiter	2.6

9. The gravity of Venus is 0.35 times that of Jupiter. What is the gravity of Venus in relation to Earth's gravity?

_____

10. How many decimal places are in the product of a number with decimal places to the hundredths multiplied by a number with decimal places to the tenths?

    A 2   **B** 3   **C** 4   **D** 5

11. Explain how you know the number of decimal places that should be in the product when you multiply two decimal numbers together.

_____

_____

_____

_____

Problem Solving:
Multiple-Step Problems

Faye is putting together packets of colored beads
to give as gifts. The chart shows the beads she
had on hand yesterday. This morning she bought
4 boxes of yellow beads containing 45 beads each.
How many packets of 60 beads can she put together?

Trinket Beads	
Color	Number
Red	195
Blue	170
Green	175

Find the hidden question or questions.

1. How many yellow beads are there?

1. $45 \times 4 = 180$

2. How many beads are there in all?

2. $195 + 170 + 175 + 180 = 720$

Solve.

$720 \div 60 = 12$

Write the answer in a sentence.

Faye will make 12 packets.

Look Back and Check

Is the answer reasonable?

Yes. Since $60 \times 10 = 600$, the

answer is reasonable.

1. Faye decides to double the number of yellow beads in
the mix. How many packets will she make if she fills
each packet with 60 beads? _____

2. **Explain It** Suppose Faye plans to fill packets with 60 beads
after deciding not to add any yellow beads to the mix. If you
want to find how many packets she can put together, what
hidden question or questions would you have to ask? Explain.

_____

_____

Name _____

Problem Solving:
Multiple-Step Problems

Write and answer the hidden question. Then solve.

1. Gloria talked on her cell phone for 320 minutes the first
   month, 243 minutes the second month, and 489 minutes
   the third month. Her payment package does not allow her
   to pay per minute; she can only buy packages. If she has
   to pay $25 for every 200 minutes, how much did she pay
   for the first three months?

   _____

   _____

   _____

   _____

2. Each can of paint will cover 450 tiles. Augustin is painting
   300 tiles in his bathroom, 675 in his kitchen, and 100 in his
   hallway. How many cans of paint does he need to buy?

   _____

   _____

3. The sum of three different numbers is 18. If every number is a
   prime number, what are the three numbers?

   _____

   _____

4. You earn $3 an hour as a waitress. After working 3 hours, you
   earn $12, $5, and $7 in tips. How much money did you earn
   in total? Explain how you found your answer.

   _____

   _____

Dividing Decimals
by 10, 100, or 1,000

You can use place-value patterns when you divide a decimal by 10, 100, or 1,000.

Sanjai has 27.5 lb of clay. If he uses the clay to make 10 bowls, how much clay will he use for each bowl? What if he makes 100 bowls from the clay? What if he makes 1,000 bowls?

Dividing a number by 10 moves the decimal point one place to the left.

$27.5 \div 10 = 2.75$

Dividing a number by 100 moves the decimal point two places to the left.

$27.5 \div 100 = 0.275$

Dividing a number by 1,000 moves the decimal point three places to the left.

$27.5 \div 1,000 = 0.0275$

Sanjai will use 2.75 lb for each of 10 bowls, 0.275 lb for each of 100 bowls, and 0.0275 lb for each of 1,000 bowls.

Remember: When you divide a number by 10, 100, or 1,000, your quotient will be smaller than that number.

For questions **1** through **6**, find the quotient. Use mental math.

1. $16.4 \div 10$ **2.** $38.92 \div 100$ **3.** $297.1 \div 100$

4. $540.9 \div 10$ **5.** $41.628 \div 1,000$ **6.** $0.33 \div 10$

7. The city has a section of land 3,694.7 ft long. The city wants to make 100 equal-sized gardens with this land. How long will each garden be?

_____

8. Connor divided 143.89 by 100. He said his answer was 14.389. Is this a reasonable answer?

_____

_____

_____

Dividing Decimals
by 10, 100, or 1,000

Find each quotient. Use mental math.

1. $86.6 \div 10 =$ _____

2. $192.5 \div 100 =$ _____

3. $1.99 \div 100 =$ _____

4. $0.87 \div 10 =$ _____

5. $228.55 \div 1,000 =$ _____

6. $0.834 \div 100 =$ _____

7. $943.35 \div 1,000 =$ _____

8. $1.25 \div 10 =$ _____

Write 10, 100, or 1,000 for each n.

9. $78.34 \div n = 0.7834$

10. $0.32 \div n = 0.032$

11. $(75.34 - 25.34) \div n = 5$

_____   _____   _____

12. There are 145 children taking swimming lessons at the pool. If 10 children will be assigned to each instructor, how many instructors need to be hired?

_____

13. Ronald ran 534.3 mi in 100 days. If he ran an equal distance each day, how many miles did he run per day?

A 5   **B** 5.13   **C** 5.343   **D** 6.201

14. Carlos says that $17.43 \div 100$ is the same as 174.3×0.01. Is he correct? Explain.

_____

_____

Estimating Decimal Quotients

When estimating with decimal division, you can use compatible numbers to make the math easier. By rounding the dividend and the divisor to numbers that can easily be divided, you will make your math computation easier.

Estimate 88.95 ÷ 0.95.

88.95 ÷ 0.95 = ?   Write the original problem.

↓   ↓

90 ÷ 0.90 = 100   Write compatible numbers.

For questions 1-4, estimate the quotients.

1. 12.72 ÷ 3.6 _____

2. 9.39 ÷ 0.92 _____

3. 0.74 ÷ .08 _____

4. 145.22 ÷ 50.2 _____

5. Mario and three friends purchased a snow blower to share. If the snow blower costs $439.20, describe how you estimate how much each person will pay?

_____

_____

_____

_____

_____

6. Is 100 a reasonable estimate for 915.25 ÷ 88.22?

_____

_____

_____

Name _____

Estimating Decimal Quotients

Use compatible numbers to find each quotient.

1. 2.90 ÷ 29 _____

2. 0.65 ÷ 5.1 _____

3. 48 ÷ 3.2 _____

4. 18.2 ÷ 11 _____

5. 0.18 ÷ 0.33 _____

6. 55 ÷ 10.7 _____

7. 152 ÷ 5.12 _____

8. 117.8 ÷ 0.12 _____

9. 41.9 ÷ 19 _____

10. 0.6 ÷ 5 _____

11. 33.90 ÷ 10.2 _____

12. 145 ÷ 0.3 _____

13. 502 ÷ 9.5 _____

14. 435.2 ÷ 39 _____

15. 180.8 ÷ 6 _____

16. 60 ÷ 5.9 _____

17. 48 ÷ 3.33 _____

18. 1.8 ÷ 20 _____

19. Martin is saving for a gaming system. The total cost of the gaming system and three games is $325.49. About how much money should he save per week to purchase the gaming system and games in 10 weeks?

    A About $0.33

    B About $3.30

    C About $33.00

    D About $330.00

20. Kayla works as a hairdresser. She earned $248.50 in tips in five days. If she earned the same amount each day, about how much did Kayla earn per day? Explain your answer.

_____

_____

_____

Number Sense: Decimal Division

You have learned how to estimate when dividing with decimals. You can also use number sense to place the decimal point in the quotient.

How many quarters are in $3.50?

When you divide decimals by decimals, you can just divide the decimals as if they are whole numbers. After finding the quotient, place the decimal by estimation.

$3.50 ÷ 0.25 = ?   Write the original problem

350 ÷ 25 = 14   Whole-number division

Place the decimal: 14.   Use estimation

How many quarters are in $3.50? _____

For questions **1-4**, place the decimal correctly.

1. $9.72 ÷ 3.6 = 2\ 7$ _____   2. $6.39 ÷ 0.72 = 8\ 8\ 7\ 5$ _____

3. $0.81 ÷ 0.09 = 9\ 0$ _____   4. $1.08 ÷ 0.27 = 4\ 0$ _____

5. Nathan and Jorge are working on a decimal division problem in math class. After finishing the problem, it looked like this: $4.76 ÷ 2.5 = 0.19$. Nathan said that the decimal is incorrectly placed in the quotient, and Jorge disagrees. Who is right? Explain your answer.

_____

_____

_____

6. Is 1.72 a reasonable answer for $86.25 ÷ 0.5$?

_____

_____

Number Sense: Decimal Division

Use estimation to place each decimal point.

1. 7.84 ÷ 0.28 = 2 8 0 _____

2. 0.65 ÷ 0.13 = 0 5 0 _____

3. 0.144 ÷ 1.2 = 1 2 0 _____

4. 9.61 ÷ 31 = 0 3 1 _____

5. 25.2 ÷ 0.42 = 0 6 0 _____

6. 8.4 ÷ 0.2 = 4 2 _____

7. 14.74 ÷ 2.2 = 6 7 0 _____

8. 28.9 ÷ 0.17 = 1 7 0 _____

9. 48.4 ÷ 0.22 = 2 2 0 _____

10. 7.6 ÷ 3.3 = 2 3 0 _____

11. 101.6 ÷ 6.8 = 1 4 9 4 _____

12. 0.148 ÷ 0.2 = 0 7 4 _____

13. 9.6 ÷ 0.12 = 0 8 0 _____

14. 75.15 ÷ 15.12 = 4 9 7 _____

15. 9.824 ÷ 3.2 = 3 0 7 _____

16. 0.93 ÷ 31 = 0 0 3 0 _____

17. 9.824 ÷ 14.69 = 1 5 5 _____

18. 11.56 ÷ 0.34 = 0 3 4 0 _____

19. Mr. Harrison bought 42 kilograms of salt for his science
classes. Each group needs 0.75 kilograms of salt for their
experiment. How many groups does Mr. Harrison have in his
science classes?

   A 0.56   **B** 5.6   **C** 56   **D** 560

20. Roman and Ranjan each divided 3.56 by 0.72. Roman got
4.94 for his quotient. Ranjan got 0.04 for his quotient. Which
student divided correctly? How do you know?

   _____

   _____

   _____

Name _____

Dividing by a Whole Number

Find 196 ÷ 32.

Step 1

Put the decimal point in the dividend. Divide. Put the decimal in the quotient right above the decimal in the dividend. Subtract.

```
      6.
32 ) 196.
    -192
       4
```

Step 2

Add a zero after the decimal point in the dividend. Bring down the zero. Divide. Subtract.

```
       6.1
32 ) 196.0
    -192 ↓
        4 0
       -3 2
          8
```

Step 3

Repeat Step 2 until there is no remainder.

```
        6.125
32 ) 196.000
    -192 ↓
        4 0
       -3 2 ↓
          80
         -64 ↓
          160
         -160
            0
```

Remember, you can use estimation to see if your answer is reasonable: 180 ÷ 30 = 6. You can check your answer using multiplication: 32 × 6.125 = 196

Find the quotient.

1. 11)93.5

2. 25)1.75

3. 6)573

_____   _____   _____

4.
```
      6.
3 ) 18.6
   -18
     0
```

5.
```
       3.
7 ) 22.61
   -21
```

6.
```
      $ 3.
12 )$44.40
   - 36
      8
```

_____   _____   _____

7. Cherri said that 0.9 ÷ 3 = 0.3. Is she correct? Explain why or why not.

_____

_____

_____

Name _____

Dividing by a Whole Number

Find the quotient.

1. $42.78 ÷ 3

_____

2. 66.5 ÷ 5

_____

3. 8.4 ÷ 10

_____

4. 5 ÷ 500

_____

5. 59.6 ÷ 4

_____

6. 188.4 ÷ 30

_____

7. $1.25 ÷ 5

_____

8. 235 ÷ 40

_____

9. 11.8 ÷ 25

_____

10. Jorge bought 6 tickets to a concert for $324. What was the cost of each ticket?

_____

11. Tony bought a 72-ounce box of dog biscuits.
How many pounds of dog biscuits did he buy?
(Remember: 1 pound = 16 ounces.)

A 4 pounds

B 4.5 pounds

C 90 pounds

D 4,320 pounds

12. Janell uses 66 beads for each necklace she makes. She bought a bag of 500 beads. How many necklaces can she make?

_____

13. In what place is the first digit of the quotient for 18.88 ÷ 4?
Tell how you know.

_____

_____

Name _____

Dividing a Whole Number by a Decimal

To divide a whole number by a decimal, multiply both numbers by a power of 10 to make the divisor a whole number.

Divide: 138 ÷ 0.04

Multiply by 100 to make 0.04 a whole number. Remember to multiply 138 by 100, too.

$$0.04 \times 100 = 4 \qquad\qquad 138 \times 100 = 13{,}800$$

Use long division to find the quotient:

```
      3,450
4)13,800
   12
    1 8
    1 6
      20
      20
```

So, 138 ÷ 0.04 = 3,450.

Use long division to find each quotient.

1. 0.3)780 _____

2. 0.5)406 _____

3. 0.02)1140 _____

4. 0.06)282 _____

5. 0.08)312 _____

6. 0.04)619 _____

Find each quotient.

7. 154 ÷ 0.7 _____

8. 3510 ÷ 0.9 _____

9. 228 ÷ 0.3 _____

10. 467 ÷ 0.02 _____

11. 106 ÷ 0.05 _____

12. 581 ÷ 0.04 _____

13. 3900 ÷ 0.08 _____

14. 207 ÷ 0.03 _____

15. 721 ÷ 0.25 _____

16. A kitchen floor has an area of 48 square feet. One tile covers 0.75 square foot. How many tiles would be needed to cover the entire kitchen floor? _____

17. Mark says that to divide 58 by 0.65, you only need to multiply both numbers by 10 because that will give you a whole number. Jan says you need to multiply both numbers by 100. Who is correct and why?

_____

_____

Name _____

Dividing a Whole Number by a Decimal

Find each quotient. Show your work.

1. 0.7)‾840 _____

2. 0.3)‾1,230 _____

3. 0.05)‾281 _____

4. 0.7)‾287 _____

5. 0.6)‾135 _____

6. 0.08)‾280 _____

7. 4,530 ÷ 0.06 _____

8. 315 ÷ 0.9 _____

9. 516 ÷ 0.03 _____

10. 827 ÷ 0.2 _____

11. 45 ÷ 0.15 _____

12. 1,233 ÷ 0.09 _____

13. A 21-pound turkey was cooked for a small banquet. The caterer figures he will discard 5 pounds of bones and that each person will eat 0.8 pounds of the remaining turkey. How many people will the turkey serve?

_____

14. During a regular half-hour TV show, there are 8 minutes of commercials. If each commercial is 0.25 minutes long, how many commercials will be shown during that show?

_____

15. A machine in a deli cooks chickens by rotating them past a heat source. One rotation takes 1.75 minutes, and it takes 35 minutes to fully cook a chicken. How many rotations does it take to cook the chicken?

A 8   **B** 14   **C** 18   **D** 20

16. One pound of horsehair is divided into "pulls" to make horsehair belts. One "pull" weighs about 0.011 ounces. How many "pulls" could be made from 6 pounds of horsehair?

_____

17. When you divide a whole number by a decimal less than 1, the quotient is greater than the whole number. Why?

_____

_____

Dividing a Decimal by a Decimal

When you divide by a decimal, you need to rewrite the dividend and the divisor so that you are dividing by a whole number.

Find $4.96 \div 0.8$.

Step 1: Estimate. Use compatible numbers.

$480 \div 80 = 6$

Step 2: Make the divisor a whole number. Multiply the divisor AND the dividend by the same power of 10.

Place the decimal point in the quotient.

$0.8 \overline{)4.96}$

$0.8 \times 10 = 8$
$4.96 \times 10 = 49.6$

Step 3: Divide as you would with whole numbers. Remember that sometimes you may need to annex zeros to complete your division.

$8 \overline{)49.6} \longrightarrow \begin{array}{r} 6.2 \\ 8\overline{)49.6} \\ \underline{48} \\ 16 \\ \underline{16} \\ 0 \end{array}$

Step 4: Compare the quotient with your estimate.

Because 6.2 is close to 6, the answer checks.

Find each quotient.

1. $0.02 \overline{)1.5}$ Estimate: _____

    Multiply dividend and divisor by what power of 10? _____

    Place the decimal point in the quotient.

    Divide. How many zeros do you need to annex? _____

    Compare the quotient to your estimate.
    Is the answer reasonable? _____

2. $0.06 \overline{)0.36}$ 3. $0.04 \overline{)9.6}$ 4. $0.75 \overline{)0.03}$

5. Fernando used tenths grids to draw this picture showing $1.6 \div 0.4 = 4$. Draw a picture to show $1.8 \div 0.6$. Write the quotient.

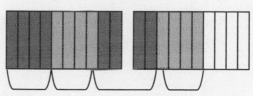

Dividing a Decimal by a Decimal

Find each quotient.

1. $8.4 \div 0.03 =$ _____

2. $66.15 \div 0.063 =$ _____

3. $100.5 \div 1.5 =$ _____

4. $860 \div 0.04 =$ _____

5. $72.8 \div 10.4 =$ _____

6. $14.36 \div 0.04 =$ _____

7. $2.87 \div 0.1 =$ _____

8. $78.2 \div 0.2 =$ _____

9. How does multiplying both the dividend and the divisor by a factor of 10 sometimes make a problem easier to solve?

_____

_____

For each item, find how many times greater the 2011 cost is than the 1955 cost. Round your answer to the nearest hundredth.

Item	1955 Cost	2011 Cost
Movie admission	$0.75	$9.50
Regular popcorn	$0.25	$4.25
Regular drink	$0.35	$2.75

10. movie admission

11. regular popcorn

12. regular drink

_____   _____   _____

13. Which item has increased the greatest amount of times from its original cost? _____

14. Divide. Round to the nearest hundredth. $250.6 \div 1.6$

   A 156   **B** 156.6   **C** 156.61   **D** 156.63

15. Allison and Rhea got different quotients when they divided 4.80 by 0.12. Whose work is correct? Explain why.

                                                             Allison   Rhea

$$\begin{array}{r} 0.40 \\ 12\overline{)4.80} \end{array} \qquad \begin{array}{r} 40.0 \\ 12\overline{)480} \end{array}$$

_____

_____

Problem Solving: Multiple-Step Problems

A multiple-step problem is a problem where you may need more than one step to find your answer.

Marcie was in a 3-day charity walk. Her friend Gayle said she would give the charity $1.50 for each mile that Marcie walked. The first day, Marcie walked 26.42 miles. The second day, Marcie walked 32.37 miles. The third day, Marcie walked 28.93 miles. How much money did Gayle give?

Step 1. Read through the problem again and write a list of what you already know.

Marcie walked 26.42, 32.37, and 28.93 miles.
Gayle gave $1.50 for each mile.

Step 2. Write a list of what you *need* to know.

Total amount Gayle gave

Step 3. Write a list of the steps to solve the problem.

Find the total number of miles Marcie walked.
Find the amount Gayle gave.

Step 4. Solve the problem one step at a time.

26.42 + 32.37 + 28.93 = 87.72   *total number of miles Marcie walked*

87.72 × $1.50 = $131.58   *total amount Gayle gave*

Use the information above to answer Exercise **1**.

1. Marcie's brother Tom was also in the charity walk. He only walked 0.8 as far as Marcie on the first day, 0.7 as far on the second day, and 0.9 as far on the third day. How many miles did Tom walk, rounded to the nearest hundredth of a mile?

_____

2. Diego is buying fruit at the store. Which costs less: 1 pound of each fruit or 4 pounds of peaches?

_____

Fruit	Cost per pound
Apples	$0.89
Oranges	$1.29
Peaches	$0.99
Grapes	$1.09

Problem Solving:
Multiple-Step Problems

Write and answer the hidden question or questions
in each problem and then solve the problem.
Write your answer in a complete sentence.

Storewide Sale	
Jeans	$29.95 for 1 pair OR 2 pairs for $55.00
T-shirts	$9.95 for 1 OR 3 T-shirts for $25.00

1. Sue bought 2 pairs of jeans and a belt that
   cost $6.95. The tax on the items was $5.85.
   Sue paid the cashier $70.00. How much money
   did Sue receive in change?

   _____

2. A recreation department purchased 12 T-shirts for day camp.
   The department does not have to pay sales tax. It paid with a
   $100.00 bill. How much change did it receive?

   _____

   _____

3. When Mrs. Johnson saw the sale, she decided to get clothes
   for each child in her family. She bought each of her 6 children
   a pair of jeans and a T-shirt. She paid $14.35 in sales tax.
   How much was Mrs. Johnson's total bill?

   A $94.35   **B** $119.70   **C** $229.35   **D** $253.35

4. Write a two-step problem that contains a hidden question about
   buying something at the mall. Tell what the hidden question is and
   solve your problem. Use $8.95 somewhere in your equation. Write
   your answer in a complete sentence.

   _____

5. What are hidden questions and why are they important when
   solving multiple-step problems?

   _____

   _____

Using Variables to Write Expressions

A variable represents a quantity that can change. To use a variable to write an algebraic expression for a situation, you need to decide which operation is appropriate for the situation. To help you, some words and phrases are listed below.

Word phrase	Variable	Operation	Algebraic Expression
ten **more than** a number *b*	*b*	Addition	*b* + 10
the **sum** of 8 and a number *c*	*c*		8 + *c*
five **less than** a number *d*	*d*	Subtraction	*d* − 5
15 **decreased by** a number *e*	*e*		15 − *e*
the **product** of 8 and a number *f*	*f*	Multiplication	8*f*
19 **times** a number *g*	*g*		19*g*
a number *h* **divided by** 2	*h*	Division	*h* ÷ 2
a number *i* **divided into** 50	*i*		50 ÷ *i*

Write each algebraic expression.

1. a number *k* **divided by** 6

   Identify the operation. _____   Write the expression. _____

2. the **sum** of 8 and a number *q*_____   3. 5 **times** a number *b* _____

4. a number *j* **divided into** 3 _____   5. 7 **less than** a number *d* _____

6. *n* fewer carrots than 12 _____   7. *w* lunches at $9 each _____

8. A touchdown scores 6 points. Write an algebraic expression to represent the number of points the Hawks will score from touchdowns.

   Identify the operation _____   Write the expression. _____

9. Write an algebraic expression to represent the situation below. Explain how the expression relates to the situation.

   Some children share 6 oranges equally among themselves.

   _____

   _____

Using Variables to Write Expressions

Write each algebraic expression.

1. 5 more than a number *s* _____

2. twice a number *k* _____

3. 17 less than a number *g* _____

4. the product of 8 and a number *p* _____

5. 84 divided by a number *z* _____

6. the sum of a number *t* and 31 _____

7. 7 more tickets than a number *m* _____

8. 21 fewer stars than three times a number *h* _____

9. Cassie has $12. She buys a balloon. Which expression shows how much money Cassie has left?

    A $b + 12$

    B $12 - b$

    C $12b$

    D $b \div 12$

10. A theater has main floor and box seating. The main floor can seat 14 people in each row. Another 20 people can sit in the box seats. Which expression shows how many people can be seated in the theater?

    A $20f - 14$

    B $20f + 14$

    C $14f - 20$

    D $14f + 20$

11. Heather bought enough shells to make *x* necklaces. Each necklace holds 16 shells. Heather has made 10 necklaces. Is $16x + 10$ a reasonable way to represent the number of shells that Heather has left to make necklaces with? Explain your answer.

_____

_____

_____

Name _____

Order of Operations

If you do not use the proper order of operations, you will not get the correct answer.

Evaluate $2^3 \div 2 + 3 \times 6 - (1 \times 5)$.

Step 1. Do the operations inside the parentheses.

$(1 \times 5) = 5$
$2^3 \div 2 + 3 \times 6 - 5$

Step 2. Evaluate any terms with exponents.

$2^3 = 8$
$8 \div 2 + 3 \times 6 - 5$

Step 3. Multiply and divide in order from left to right.

$8 \div 2 = 4$ and $3 \times 6 = 18$
$4 + 18 - 5$

Step 4. Add and subtract in order from left to right.

$4 + 18 = 22$
$22 - 5 = 17$
So, $2^3 \div 2 + 3 \times 6 - (1 \times 5) = 17$

Write which operation should be done first.

1. $6 + 3 \times 2$ _____

2. $13 - 1 + 4 \div 2$ _____

3. $5 \times (7 - 2) + 1$ _____

4. $(19 + 23) - (4 \times 5)$ _____

For questions **5** through **8**, evaluate the expression for $x = 6$ and $y = 17$.

5. $4x + 5y$ _____

6. $2x + (20 - y)$ _____

7. $x \div 3 + y$ _____

8. $4y \div 2 + (8x + 10)$ _____

9. Patty made $34 baby sitting on each of 3 weekends. If she spent $50 on gifts for her family, how much money does she have left?

_____

10. Carlos solved $20 - (2 \times 6) + 8 \div 4 = 29$. Is this the correct answer?

_____

_____

Order of Operations

Use the order of operations to evaluate each expression.

1. $4 \times 4 + 3 =$ _____

2. $3 + 6 \times 2 \div 3 =$ _____

3. $24 - (8 \div 2) + 6 =$ _____

4. $(15 - 11) \times (25 \div 5) =$ _____

5. $26 - 4 \times 5 + 2 =$ _____

6. $15 \times (7 - 7) + (5 \times 2) =$ _____

7. $(8 \div 4) \times (7 \times 0) =$ _____

8. $5 \times (6 - 3) + 10 \div (8 - 3) =$ _____

9. Which is a true statement, $5 \times 4 + 1 = 25$ or $3 + 7 \times 2 = 17$?
Explain your answer.

_____

_____

Insert parentheses to make each statement true.

10. $25 \div 5 - 4 = 25$ _____

11. $7 \times 4 - 4 \div 2 = 26$ _____

12. $3 + 5 \times 2 - 10 = 6$ _____

13. Insert parentheses in the expression
$6 + 10 \times 2$ so that:

a. the expression equals 32. _____

b. the expression equals $(12 + 1) \times 2$. _____

14. Solve $(25 - 7) \times 2 \div 4 + 2$.

A 18 B 11 C 6 D 5

15. Write two order-of-operation problems. Then trade with a
classmate and solve the problems.

_____

_____

Simplifying Expressions

When an expression contains more than one operation, **parentheses ( )** can be used to show which computation should be done. Parentheses are one type of **grouping symbol**.

Do the computation inside the parentheses first.

Evaluate $(2 + 8) \times 3$.

$$10 \quad \times 3 = 30$$

Evaluate $2 + (8 \times 3)$.

$$2 + \quad 24 = 26$$

Some expressions contain more than one set of parentheses.

Do the computation inside each pair of parentheses first.

Evaluate $(4 + 9) - (30 \div 5)$.

$$13 \quad - \quad 6 = 7$$

After you solve the computations inside the parentheses, use the order of operations to choose which computation to solve next:

Exponents

Multiplication and division from left to right

Addition and subtraction from left to right

---

1. $(16 + 4) \div 10$

2. $(16 \div 4) + (10 - 3)$

3. $8^2 \div (2 \times 4)$

_____

_____

_____

4. $27 - (5 \times 3)$

5. $(4 \times 6) \div 6 + 6$

6. $(36 \div 6) \times 2^2$

_____

_____

_____

7. Evaluate $11 \times (8 - n)$ for $n = 4$. _____

Name _____

Simplifying Expressions

1. $(18 \div 9) + 7$

2. $(4 + 3) \times (9 - 2)$

3. $32 \div (8 + 8)$

_____

_____

_____

4. $(26 - 17) \times (9 \div 3)$

5. $64 \div (5 + 1 + 2)$

6. $27 \div (3 \times 3) + 7$

_____

_____

_____

Rewrite with parentheses to make each sentence true.

7. $42 + 12 \div 6 = 44$ _____

8. $33 - 14 + 4 = 15$ _____

9. $32 \div 8 \times 2 = 8$ _____

Evaluate each expression for $w = 9$.

10. $72 \div (w + 0)$

11. $(12 + w) \div 3$

12. $(0 + w) \times 2$

_____

_____

_____

13. Write an expression to show how much Gretchen paid for drama, action, and comedy videos if she paid $4 each at a sale.

Gretchen's Video Purchases	
Mystery	6
Action	3
Comedy	5
Drama	2
Romance	2

_____

14. Which statement is true when $x = 7$?

A $63 \div x = 21$

C $0 \div x = 7$

B $(x - 6) - (1 \times 1) = 1$

D $(2 + 7) \times (12 - x) = 45$

15. Evaluate the expression $7 + (32 \div 16) \times 4 - 6$. What steps did you use to find the answer?

_____

_____

Evaluating Expressions

Brackets and parentheses are both used to show groupings.
Brackets are used to avoid double parentheses: [(instead of ((.

Evaluate expressions according to the order of operations.

1. Evaluate inside parentheses, then evaluate inside brackets.	$2.3^2 + [(9 \times 0.4) + (3 \times 0.8)] \times 1.2$ $2.3^2 + [3.6 + 2.4] \times 1.2$ $2.3^2 + 6 \times 1.2$
2. Evaluate terms with exponents.	$2.3^2 + 6 \times 1.2$ $5.29 + 6 \times 1.2$
3. Multiply and divide from left to right.	$5.29 + 6 \times 1.2$ $5.29 + 7.2$
4. Add and subtract from left to right.	$5.29 + 7.2$ 12.49

Evaluate each expression.

1. $(4.8 \div 2) \times 5$

_____

2. $3.6 + (3 \times 9.6 - 4.8)$

_____

3. $[(6.2 \times 8.4) - 9.28]$

_____

4. $[7 \times (9.6 \div 3)] + 12.4$

_____

5. $6 \times [(6 \times 2.3) + 3.9]$

_____

6. $2^4 \div [(3.35 \times 0.8) + 5.32]$

_____

7. $9.6 + [(3.1 \times 2) - 2.3] + 4^2$

_____

8. $6^2 - 9 \div [(0.24 \times 5) + (0.66 \times 5)]$

_____

9. How would you use estimation to evaluate this expression:
$10.2 \times [(2 \times 3.7) + 8]$?

_____

Name _____

Evaluating Expressions

1. $5^2 - (3.1 \times 6 + 5.3)$

_____

2. $4^2 - [(4.2 \times 3.5) - 9.5]$

_____

3. $3^2 - [(12 - 2^2) \times 0.6]$

_____

4. $[(0.2 \times 8) + (2.5 \times 3)] + 5^2$

_____

5. $42 \div [8.6 - (8 \times 0.2)]$

_____

6. $3^3 + 4.2 \times 8 \div 0.2$

_____

7. $6.8 + [(0.5 \times 7) + (3.1 \times 3)]$

_____

8. $5^2 - [(6^2 - 32.4) + (8 \div 0.5)] + 4.5$

_____

9. $9 + [(4.2 - 3.3) + (6.4 \div 0.8)] \times 3$

_____

10. $41 - 3^2 + (8 \times 2.3) - 15 + (2.1 \times 4)$

_____

11. Keisha bought a new pair of skis for $450. She put $120 down and got a student discount of $45. Her mother gave her $\frac{1}{2}$ of the balance for her birthday. Which of these expressions could be used to find the amount Keisha still owes on the skis?

A $450 - 120 + 45 \div 2$

C $450 - (120 - 45) \div 2$

B $[450 - (120 - 45) \div 2]$

D $[450 - (120 + 45)] \div 2$

12. $(7 \times 3.4) - [(2.8 \times 5) - (4.3 \times 2)] + 4^2$. Give the order of operations a student solving this problem would use to evaluate the expression. Solve.

_____

_____

Name _____

Addition and Subtraction Expressions

How do you find a rule to write an expression?

To find a rule and write an expression, look at the numbers being compared. Which is the greater number?

Consider 57 and 50. 57 is greater than 50, so rule out addition.

Find how much greater 57 is than 50. 57 is 7 more than 50, so the rule must involve subtraction.

Look at the other two columns of numbers and compare them. The top number is 7 more than the bottom number.

A rule is subtract 7, so the expression is $v - 7$.

v	57	28	10
	50	21	3

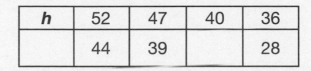

Compare the numbers in each column of the table.

Find a rule for each table.

1.

r	24	28	31	36
	11	15	18	23

2.

f	17	41	86	93
	21	45	90	97

Find a rule and write the missing number for each table.

3.

c	7	10	15	19
	32	35		44

4.

h	52	47	40	36
	44	39		28

5.

m	68	72	77	82
	25		34	39

6.

s	34	37	74	78
	51	54	91	

Addition and Subtraction Expressions

Find a rule and write the missing number for each table.

1.

r	19	24	32	37
	7	12	20	

2.

a		6	9	12	15
		40		46	49

3.

s	10	15	25	30
	5	10		25

4.

b	16	19	22	26
		35	38	42

5.

w	3	6	9	12
	6		12	15

6.

n	51	42	33	24
	40	31		13

7. Evaluate the expression $15 - n$ when $n = 9$. _____

8. Which expression stands for "32 more than a number d"?

    A $32 \times d$

    B $32 - d$

    C $32 + d$

    D $32 \div d$

9. Explain what the variable represents in an addition or subtraction expression.

_____

_____

_____

Multiplication and Division Expressions

Find a rule and write an expression using multiplication and division.

To find a rule and write an expression, look at the numbers being compared. Which is the greater number?

b	3	6	8
	24	48	64

Compare the numbers in each column of the table.

Consider 3 and 24. Because 24 is greater than 3, you can rule out subtraction and division.

Find how much greater 24 is than 3. Since 24 is 8 times 3, the rule must involve multiplication.

Look at the other two columns of numbers and compare them. The bottom number is 8 times as great as the top number.

A rule is multiply by 8, so the expression is $8 \times b$.

Find a rule for each table.

1.

a	48	56	64	72
	6	7	8	9

2.

u	8	11	13	16
	32	44	52	64

Find a rule and write the missing number for each table.

3.

j	18	14	12	8
	9	7		4

4.

e	2	4	6	7
	6	12	18	

5.

p	4	6	10	17
	20		50	85

6.

q	48	42	30	24
	8		5	4

Name _____

Multiplication and Division Expressions

Find a rule and write the missing number for each table.

1.

m	6	7	8	9
	54	63		81

2.

k	14	21	49	63
	2	3		9

3.

z	24	18	9	0
	8		3	0

4.

q	2	3	4	5
	14	21	28	

5.

e	5	7	9	11
		42	54	66

6.

l	64	48	32	24
	8	6	4	

7.

s	3	8	10	16
	60	160		320

8.

d	30	25	15	5
		5	3	1

9. Evaluate the expression 48 ÷ *n* when *n* = 6. _____

10. Which expression means "3 times a number *h*"?

   A $3 \times h$ **B** $3 - h$ **C** $3 + h$ **D** $3 \div h$

11. How could you change Exercise 5 so that your rule uses the inverse operation?

_____

_____

_____

Patterns: Extending Tables

Sometimes a rule tells us how to create a sequence of numbers.

Rule A: Start with 0. Add 5.

Rule B: Start with 0. Add 15.

We can use a table to collect the sequences, and find a corresponding relationship between the terms.

	Start	First Term	Second Term	Third Term
Rule A	0	5	10	15
Rule B	0	15	30	45

Look for a way in which the numbers in each column are related. Each term from Rule B is 3 times as great as the corresponding term in Rule A.

In **1–4**, fill in the tables and find the relationship between the corresponding terms.

1. **Rule A:** Start with 20. Subtract 2.   **Rule B:** Start with 40. Subtract 2.

	Start	First Term	Second Term	Third Term
Rule A	20	18	16	
Rule B	40	38	36	

2. **Rule C:** Start with 30. Add 5.   **Rule D:** Start with 50. Add 5.

	Start	First Term	Second Term	Third Term
Rule C	30	35		
Rule D	50	55		

3. **Rule G:** Start with 0. Add 2.   **Rule H:** Start with 0. Add 10.

	Start	First Term	Second Term	Third Term
Rule G				
Rule H				

Patterns: Extending Tables

In **1–3**, fill in the tables and find the relationship between the corresponding terms.

1. Rule A: Start with 40. Subtract 5.   **Rule B:** Start with 63. Subtract 5.

	Start	First Term	Second Term	Third Term
Rule A	40	35		
Rule B	63	58		

2. Rule C: Start with 64. Divide by 4.   **Rule D:** Start with 128. Divide by 4.

	Start	First Term	Second Term	Third Term
Rule C	64			
Rule D	128			

3. Rule G: Start with 3. Multiply by 2.   **Rule H:** Start with 6. Multiply by 2.

	Start	First Term	Second Term	Third Term
Rule G				
Rule H				

In **4–7,** find the relationship between the corresponding terms in each rule.

4. Rule A: Start with 47. Subtract 3.

   Rule B: Start with 59. Subtract 3.

5. Rule A: Start with 9. Add 4.

   Rule B: Start with 22. Add 4.

6. Rule A: Start with 6. Multiply by 2.

   Rule B: Start with 18. Multiply by 2.

7. Rule A: Start with 64. Divide by 2.

   Rule B: Start with 256. Divide by 2.

Variables and Expressions

A **variable** is a letter or symbol. It represents an unknown amount that can change.

You can do mathematical operations with variables and numbers.

You can state these operations in word expressions. You can also state them in algebraic expressions.

Operation	+	−	×	÷
Word expression	the sum of r and 3	the difference between r and 3	the product of r and 3	r divided by 3
Algebraic expression	$r + 3$	$r − 3$	$3r$	$r ÷ 3$
Other ways of saying the word expression	3 added to r 3 more than r	3 subtracted from r 3 less than r	r multiplied by 3 3 times r	r separated into 3 equal parts

Complete the algebraic expression for each of the following word expressions.

1. the sum of b and 8

b ____ 8

2. the difference between m and 6

m ____ 6

3. the quotient of k and 16

k ____ 16

4. 7 less than z

z ____ 7

5. 2 more than d

d ____ 2

6. j divided by 4

j ____ 4

Circle the letter of the correct word expression for each algebraic expression.

7. $t − 13$ a. 13 subtracted from t b. t subtracted from 13

8. $4n$ a. 4 more than n b. 4 times n

9. $11 + s$ a. 11 more than s b. 11 less than s

10. $45a$ a. the product of a and 45   b. 45 more than a

11. $y ÷ 6$ a. y less 6   b. 6 equal parts of y

12. $v − 5$ a. 5 less than v b. v subtracted from 5

Variables and Expressions

For questions **1** through **4**, use a variable to write an algebraic expression that represents the word phrase.

1. a number of apples divided into 12 baskets _____

2. 5 more than *s* _____

3. three times the cost for one hat _____

4. nine fewer than the total number of people _____

For **5** through **7**, translate each algebraic expression into words.

5. $3 + w$ _____

6. $8x$ _____

7. $40 - p$ _____

8. Write two different word phrases for the expression $\frac{t}{30}$.

_____

_____

9. Do $5 + x$ and $x + 5$ represent the same expression? Explain.

_____

_____

10. Dan is 12 in. taller than Jay. Use *x* for Jay's height. Which expression shows Dan's height?

    A $x + 12$ **B** $x - 12$ **C** $12x$ **D** $\frac{x}{12}$

11. Explain what the expression $6x$ means.

_____

Problem Solving: Act It Out and Use Reasoning

In Mackenzie's class there are 23 students. 14 students have brown hair. 2 times as many students have blonde hair as have red hair. How many students have each color hair?

Draw a diagram to show what you know.

There are 9 students left. You know that two times as many have blonde hair as have red hair. Make a table to try different numbers and see which pair fits the problem.

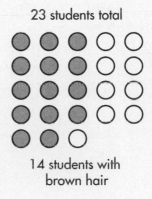

23 students total

14 students with brown hair

red		blonde	Do numbers add up to 9?
1	$1 \times 2 =$	2	does not equal 9
2	$2 \times 2 =$	4	does not equal 9
3	$3 \times 2 =$	6	equals 9

Since $6 = 2 \times 3$ and $6 + 3 = 9$, this is the correct answer.

So, in Mackenzie's class, there are 14 students with brown hair, 6 with blonde hair, and 3 with red hair.

In **1** and **2**, solve. Draw a picture and/or table to help find the answer.

1. Jacobson Animal Shelter has half as many cats as dogs. The shelter has 30 dogs. How many total animals does the shelter have?

   _____

2. Summer's mother gave Summer $20 to share with her 3 brothers equally. How much did each person get?

   _____

Problem Solving: Act It Out and Use Reasoning

1. Christina collects stamps. She has 47 stamps in all. She has 20 stamps from Europe. The number of African stamps is 2 times the number of Asian stamps. How many stamps from each of these three continents does she have?

_____

2. Write a problem that can be solved by acting it out and using reasoning.

_____

_____

_____

3. A public pool opened for the summer. A total of 246 people came swimming over the first 3 days it was open. On the first day, 79 came to swim. On the second day, 104 people swam. How many people swam on the third day?

_____

4. Marissa earned $480 in the summer. If she earned $40 a week, how many weeks did she work?

A 48   B 12   C 10   D 9

5. How could you use cubes to act out a problem?

_____

_____

_____

_____

Name _____

Equivalent Fractions

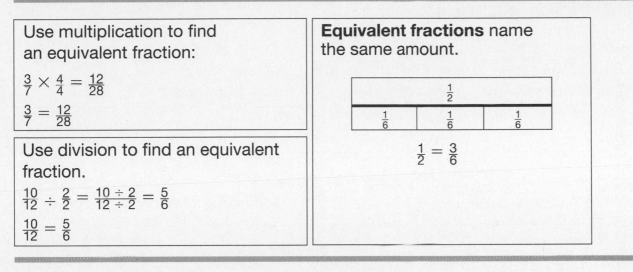

Use multiplication to find an equivalent fraction:

$\frac{3}{7} \times \frac{4}{4} = \frac{12}{28}$

$\frac{3}{7} = \frac{12}{28}$

Use division to find an equivalent fraction.

$\frac{10}{12} \div \frac{2}{2} = \frac{10 \div 2}{12 \div 2} = \frac{5}{6}$

$\frac{10}{12} = \frac{5}{6}$

Equivalent fractions name the same amount.

$\frac{1}{2} = \frac{3}{6}$

Use multiplication to find an equivalent fraction.

1. $\frac{3}{8}$ _____   2. $\frac{1}{3}$ _____   3. $\frac{4}{7}$ _____

4. $\frac{1}{2}$ _____   5. $\frac{5}{9}$ _____   6. $\frac{3}{10}$ _____

7. $\frac{8}{11}$ _____   8. $\frac{7}{16}$ _____   9. $\frac{11}{12}$ _____

Use division to find an equivalent fraction.

10. $\frac{15}{20}$ _____   11. $\frac{4}{18}$ _____   12. $\frac{15}{60}$ _____

13. $\frac{32}{40}$ _____   14. $\frac{80}{100}$ _____   15. $\frac{35}{45}$ _____

16. $\frac{15}{75}$ _____   17. $\frac{32}{48}$ _____   18. $\frac{18}{32}$ _____

Find two equivalent fractions for each given fraction.

19. $\frac{3}{6}$ _____   20. $\frac{3}{9}$ _____   21. $\frac{10}{12}$ _____

22. $\frac{75}{100}$ _____   23. $\frac{1}{2}$ _____   24. $\frac{7}{12}$ _____

25. $\frac{6}{8}$ _____   26. $\frac{20}{24}$ _____   27. $\frac{1}{8}$ _____

28. Why do you have to multiply or divide both the numerator and denominator of a fraction to find an equivalent fraction?

_____

_____

_____

Equivalent Fractions

Find two fractions equivalent to each fraction.

1. $\frac{5}{6}$ _____ 2. $\frac{10}{20}$ _____ 3. $\frac{45}{60}$ _____

4. $\frac{28}{32}$ _____ 5. $\frac{20}{8}$ _____ 6. $\frac{16}{32}$ _____

7. $\frac{36}{60}$ _____ 8. $\frac{16}{48}$ _____ 9. $\frac{2}{3}$ _____

10. Are the fractions $\frac{1}{5}$, $\frac{5}{5}$, and $\frac{5}{1}$ equivalent? Explain.

_____

11. The United States currently has 50 states. What fraction of the states had become a part of the United States by 1795? Write your answer as two equivalent fractions.

_____

12. In what year was the total number of states in the United States $\frac{3}{5}$ the number it was in 1960?

_____

Number of States in the United States

Year	Number of States
1795	15
1848	30
1900	45
1915	48
1960	50

13. Which of the following pairs of fractions are equivalent?

A $\frac{1}{10}$, $\frac{3}{33}$ B $\frac{9}{5}$, $\frac{5}{9}$ C $\frac{5}{45}$, $\frac{1}{9}$ D $\frac{6}{8}$, $\frac{34}{48}$

14. In what situation can you use only multiplication to find equivalent fractions to a given fraction? Give an example.

_____

_____

Fractions in Simplest Form

Write $\frac{20}{24}$ in simplest form. Divide by common factors.

- Divide by common factors until the only common factor is 1.

- You can start by dividing by 2, since both numbers are even.

$$\frac{20 \div 2}{24 \div 2} = \frac{10}{12}$$

But both 10 and 12 are also even, so they can be divided by 2.

$$\frac{10 \div 2}{12 \div 2} = \frac{5}{6}$$

- Since 5 and 6 do not have any common factors, $\frac{5}{6}$ is the simplest form.

$\frac{20}{24}$ written in simplest form is $\frac{5}{6}$.

Write each fraction in simplest form.

1. $\frac{16}{20}$ _____   **2.** $\frac{8}{16}$ _____   **3.** $\frac{5}{10}$ _____

4. $\frac{8}{32}$ _____   **5.** $\frac{18}{42}$ _____   **6.** $\frac{15}{100}$ _____

7. $\frac{18}{21}$ _____   **8.** $\frac{24}{40}$ _____   **9.** $\frac{55}{70}$ _____

10. Explain how you can tell that $\frac{31}{33}$ is in simplest form.

_____

_____

_____

Name _____

Fractions in Simplest Form

Write each fraction in simplest form.

1. $\frac{5}{10}$ _____

2. $\frac{6}{24}$ _____

3. $\frac{9}{27}$ _____

4. $\frac{3}{15}$ _____

5. $\frac{10}{12}$ _____

6. $\frac{9}{15}$ _____

7. $\frac{2}{18}$ _____

8. $\frac{25}{60}$ _____

9. $\frac{12}{72}$ _____

10. Explain how you can tell $\frac{4}{5}$ is in simplest form.

_____

_____

_____

Write in simplest form.

11. What fraction of the problems on
the math test will be word problems?

_____

12. What fraction of the problems on the math
test will be multiple-choice problems?   _____

Math Test
➡ 20 Multiple-choice problems
➡ 10 Fill in the blanks
➡ 5 Word problems

13. Which is the simplest form of $\frac{10}{82}$?

A $\frac{1}{8}$ B $\frac{1}{22}$ C $\frac{10}{82}$ D $\frac{5}{41}$

14. Explain how you can find the simplest form of $\frac{100}{1,000}$.

_____

_____

_____

Problem Solving: Writing to Explain

An environmental scientist is studying an old apple orchard. The orchard is shown on the right. Some of the trees are infected with mold. Other trees are infested with beetles. Some trees are normal.

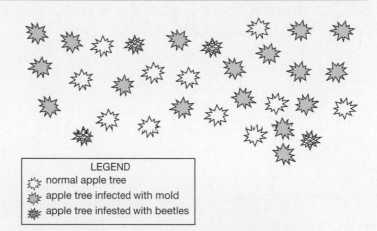

LEGEND
normal apple tree
apple tree infected with mold
apple tree infested with beetles

The scientist knows that pictures and symbols can be used to write a good math explanation. So she decides to organize her findings in the chart on the right.

Use this chart to estimate the fractional part of the orchard that is infected with mold, using a benchmark fraction that is close to the actual amount.

A little more than half the grid is covered by trees that are infected with mold.

Use this chart to estimate the fractional part of the orchard that is infested with beetles. Explain how you decided.

_____

_____

_____

Name _____

Problem Solving:
Writing to Explain

Estimate the fractional part of the shaded portions below.
Explain how you decided.

1. _____

_____

2. _____

_____

3. Draw a square and shade about $\frac{1}{8}$ of it. How did
you decide how much to shade?

_____

4. Draw two rectangles that are different sizes. Shade about $\frac{1}{2}$ of
each. Are the shaded parts the same amount? Explain.

_____

_____

5. Look at a picture of the American flag. Approximately what
part of the flag is blue? Explain.

_____

_____

Estimating Sums and Differences of Fractions

To estimate the sum or difference of two fractions, replace each fraction with the nearest half or whole. You can use a number line to check whether each fraction is closest to 0, $\frac{1}{2}$, or 1. Estimate the sum of $\frac{3}{8} + \frac{9}{16}$.

Step 1: Find $\frac{3}{8}$ on the number line. Is $\frac{3}{8}$ closer to 0 or $\frac{1}{2}$? _____

$$\frac{3}{8}$$
```
←++++++++●++++++++→
  0       1       1
          2
```

Step 2: Find $\frac{9}{16}$ on the number line. Is $\frac{9}{16}$ closer to $\frac{1}{2}$ or to 1? _____

$$\frac{9}{16}$$
```
←+++++++++●+++++++→
  0       1       1
          2
```

Step 3: Add to find the estimate. $\frac{1}{2} + \frac{1}{2} = 1$.

For **1** and **2**, complete each sentence to help you replace each fraction with the nearest half or whole. Use each number line to help.

1. $\frac{7}{8}$ is between _____ and _____ but

   is closer to _____. $\frac{7}{8}$ rounds to _____
```
←+++++++++++++→
  0     1     1
        2
```

2. $\frac{5}{16}$ is between _____ and _____ but

   is closer to _____. $\frac{5}{16}$ rounds to _____
```
←+++++++++++++++++++→
  0       1        1
          2
```

For **3** through **10**, estimate each sum or difference by replacing each fraction with 0, $\frac{1}{2}$, or 1.

3. $\frac{2}{5} + \frac{3}{4}$ 4. $\frac{7}{8} - \frac{4}{9}$ 5. $\frac{1}{2} + \frac{4}{7}$ 6. $\frac{7}{12} - \frac{4}{9}$

7. $\frac{7}{15} + \frac{6}{10}$ 8. $\frac{2}{3} - \frac{4}{8}$ 9. $\frac{2}{9} + \frac{4}{5}$ 10. $\frac{7}{8} - \frac{5}{6}$

Estimating Sums and Differences of Fractions

In **1** through **8**, tell if each fraction is closest to 0, $\frac{1}{2}$, or 1. You may use a number line to help.

1. $\frac{1}{9}$ _____

2. $\frac{5}{9}$ _____

3. $\frac{11}{20}$ _____

4. $\frac{6}{10}$ _____

5. $\frac{6}{7}$ _____

6. $\frac{5}{12}$ _____

7. $\frac{3}{4}$ _____

8. $\frac{12}{15}$ _____

In **9** through **16**, estimate each sum or difference by replacing each fraction with 0, $\frac{1}{2}$, or 1.

9. $\frac{7}{12} + \frac{4}{5}$

10. $\frac{1}{12} + \frac{2}{4}$

11. $\frac{4}{9} - \frac{1}{6}$

12. $\frac{2}{6} + \frac{8}{9}$

13. $\frac{1}{6} - \frac{1}{8}$

14. $\frac{2}{5} - \frac{3}{7}$

15. $\frac{7}{8} - \frac{7}{9}$

16. $\frac{5}{12} + \frac{2}{5}$

17. Which is the best estimate for the difference of $\frac{9}{16} - \frac{4}{9}$?

   A $1 - 1 = 0$ **C** $1 - \frac{1}{2} = \frac{1}{2}$

   B $\frac{1}{2} - \frac{1}{2} = 0$ **D** $0 - 0 = 0$

18. Which fraction can NOT be replaced with $\frac{1}{2}$ when estimating?

   A $\frac{10}{12}$ **C** $\frac{4}{10}$

   B $\frac{2}{6}$ **D** $\frac{13}{24}$

19. Mia estimated $\frac{5}{8} + \frac{1}{9}$ by replacing $\frac{5}{8}$ with 1 and $\frac{1}{9}$ with 0. Her estimated sum was $1 + 0 = 1$. Explain why Mia's estimate is NOT accurate.

_____

_____

_____

Common Multiples and Least Common Multiple

A multiple of a number is a product of a given whole number and another whole number. The first four multiples of 3 are 3, 6, 9, and 12.

A least common multiple (LCM) is the least number that is a common multiple of two or more numbers.

Find the least common multiple of 4 and 6.

4	6	Are there the same number of X's in each column? No.
XXXX	XXXXXX	Since the 1st column has fewer, add another set of 4 X's.

4	6	Are there the same number of X's in each column? No.
XXXX	XXXXXX	Since the 2nd column has fewer, add another set of 6 X's.
XXXX		

4	6	Are there the same number of X's in each column? No.
XXXX	XXXXXX	Since the 1st column has fewer, add another set of 4 X's.
XXXX	XXXXXX	

4	6	Are there the same number of X's in each column? Yes.
XXXX	XXXXXX	Since the columns are equal, the number of X's is the LCM. The LCM = 12.
XXXX	XXXXXX	
XXXX		

Find the least common multiple of each number pair.

1. 2 and 3 _____   2. 6 and 9 _____   3. 5 and 6 _____   4. 8 and 3 _____

5. Can the LCM of 9 and 17 be less than 17? Explain.

_____

_____

_____

Name _____

Common Multiples
and Least Common Multiple

Find the LCM of each pair of numbers.

1. 3 and 6 _____

2. 7 and 10 _____

3. 8 and 12 _____

4. 2 and 5 _____

5. 4 and 6 _____

6. 3 and 4 _____

7. 5 and 8 _____

8. 2 and 9 _____

9. 6 and 7 _____

10. 4 and 7 _____

11. 5 and 20 _____

12. 6 and 12 _____

13. Rosario is buying pens for school. Blue pens are sold in packages
of 6. Black pens are sold in packages of 3, and green pens are sold
in packages of 2. What is the least number of pens she can buy
to have equal numbers of pens in each color?

_____

14. A punch recipe calls for equal amounts of pineapple juice and orange
juice. Pineapple juice comes in 6-ounce cans and orange juice comes
in 10-ounce cans. What is the least amount of each kind of juice that
can be mixed without having any left over?

_____

15. Dawn ordered 4 pizzas each costing between 8 and 12 dollars.
What is a reasonable total cost of all 4 pizzas?

A Less than $24

C Between $32 and $48

B Between $12 and $24

D About $70

16. Why is 35 the LCM of 7 and 5?

_____

Name _____

Finding Common Denominators

How to find a common denominator.

Find a common denominator for $\frac{4}{10}$ and $\frac{3}{8}$.

List multiples of the denominators 10 and 8. Then look for a common multiple.

10: 10, 20, 30, 40

8: 8, 16, 24, 32, 40

The number 40 can be used as the common denominator.

How to rename fractions to have the same denominator.

Rename $\frac{4}{10}$ and $\frac{3}{8}$ using 40 as the common denominator.

Multiply the numerator and denominator by the same nonzero numbers.

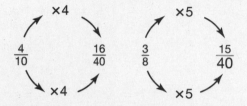

The renamed fractions are $\frac{16}{40}$ and $\frac{15}{40}$.

In **1** through **8**, find a common denominator for each pair of fractions.

1. $\frac{2}{7}$ and $\frac{1}{2}$ **2.** $\frac{4}{5}$ and $\frac{2}{3}$ **3.** $\frac{3}{4}$ and $\frac{5}{6}$ **4.** $\frac{7}{8}$ and $\frac{3}{10}$

5. $\frac{3}{4}$ and $\frac{5}{16}$ **6.** $\frac{1}{9}$ and $\frac{1}{2}$ **7.** $\frac{2}{3}$ and $\frac{1}{8}$ **8.** $\frac{7}{20}$ and $\frac{4}{15}$

In **9** through **16**, find a common denominator for each pair of fractions. Then rename each fraction in the pair.

9. $\frac{4}{10}$ and $\frac{1}{5}$ **10.** $\frac{4}{9}$ and $\frac{4}{6}$ **11.** $\frac{1}{2}$ and $\frac{1}{7}$ **12.** $\frac{2}{3}$ and $\frac{3}{18}$

13. $\frac{4}{16}$ and $\frac{2}{3}$ **14.** $\frac{1}{6}$ and $\frac{1}{4}$ **15.** $\frac{2}{20}$ and $\frac{1}{8}$ **16.** $\frac{7}{12}$ and $\frac{7}{15}$

R 9·6

Finding Common Denominators

In **1** through **8**, find a common denominator for each pair of fractions.

1. $\frac{2}{5}$ and $\frac{3}{4}$ **2.** $\frac{5}{8}$ and $\frac{4}{9}$ **3.** $\frac{1}{4}$ and $\frac{4}{7}$ **4.** $\frac{5}{12}$ and $\frac{7}{9}$

5. $\frac{7}{15}$ and $\frac{1}{3}$ **6.** $\frac{1}{2}$ and $\frac{2}{3}$ **7.** $\frac{2}{9}$ and $\frac{4}{5}$ **8.** $\frac{7}{8}$ and $\frac{5}{6}$

In **9** through **16**, find a common denominator for each pair of fractions. Then rename each fraction in the pair.

9. $\frac{3}{12}$ and $\frac{3}{8}$ **10.** $\frac{1}{8}$ and $\frac{2}{7}$ **11.** $\frac{1}{2}$ and $\frac{2}{9}$ **12.** $\frac{1}{3}$ and $\frac{1}{5}$

13. $\frac{7}{9}$ and $\frac{1}{6}$ **14.** $\frac{1}{6}$ and $\frac{3}{4}$ **15.** $\frac{7}{8}$ and $\frac{2}{3}$ **16.** $\frac{3}{8}$ and $\frac{5}{6}$

17. Train A arrives at Central Station on the hour and every 12 minutes. Train B arrives on the hour and every 15 minutes. When do both trains arrive at the same time?

   A On the hour and 30 minutes past the hour

   B On the hour and 15 minutes to the hour

   C On the hour and 27 minutes past the hour

   D On the hour only

18. Andrew wants to rename $\frac{2}{7}$ and $\frac{3}{4}$ using a common denominator. Which of the following shows these fractions renamed correctly?

   A $\frac{8}{28}$ and $\frac{21}{28}$

   B $\frac{2}{28}$ and $\frac{3}{28}$

   C $\frac{4}{28}$ and $\frac{6}{28}$

   D $\frac{2}{7}$ and $\frac{3}{7}$

19. Manuel says that you can use one of the denominators of $\frac{5}{6}$ and $\frac{11}{30}$ when renaming these fractions using a common denominator. Why is this true?

_____

_____

_____

P 9·6

Adding Fractions with Unlike Denominators

Danisha ate $\frac{2}{3}$ cup of yogurt at breakfast. She ate $\frac{1}{4}$ cup of yogurt at lunch. How much yogurt did she eat today?

You can add fractions with unlike denominators.

Step 1: Find the least common denominator of the two fractions.	Step 2: Once you have equivalent fractions with the same denominator, add the numerators.	Step 3: Place the sum over the common denominator and simplify your fraction if possible.
multiples of 3: 3, 6, 9, 12, 15 **multiples of 4:** 4, 8, 12, 16, 20 $\frac{2}{3} = \frac{8}{12}$ and $\frac{1}{4} = \frac{3}{12}$	$8 + 3 = 11$ So, $\frac{8}{12} + \frac{3}{12} = \frac{11}{12}$.	Danisha ate $\frac{11}{12}$ cup of yogurt today.

For **1** through **5**, find each sum. Simplify if possible.

1. $\begin{array}{r} \frac{3}{5} \\ + \frac{1}{6} \\ \hline \end{array}$

2. $\begin{array}{r} \frac{2}{9} \\ + \frac{2}{6} \\ \hline \end{array}$

3. $\begin{array}{r} \frac{3}{8} \\ + \frac{3}{12} \\ \hline \end{array}$

4. $\frac{1}{4} + \frac{1}{6} + \frac{3}{4} =$

5. $\frac{2}{9} + \frac{1}{9} + \frac{1}{6} =$

6. Kevin and some friends baked different loaves of bread and cut them into different numbers of slices. They ate $\frac{1}{4}$ of one loaf, $\frac{1}{4}$ of another, $\frac{5}{12}$ of another, and $\frac{1}{12}$ of another. Did they eat the equivalent of a whole loaf?

_____

7. Cathy wakes up at 7:00 A.M. each morning. She spends $\frac{1}{10}$ hour making her bed, $\frac{1}{5}$ hour eating breakfast, and $\frac{1}{2}$ hour getting ready for school. How long does Cathy spend doing these things each morning?

_____

Name _____

Adding Fractions with Unlike Denominators

Find each sum. Simplify if necessary.

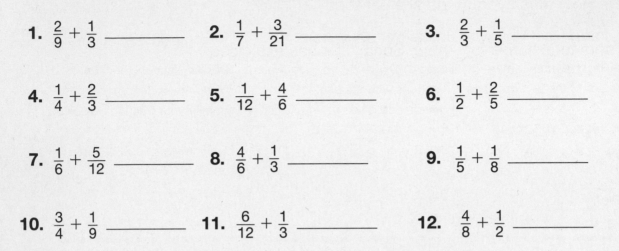

1. $\frac{2}{9} + \frac{1}{3}$ _____ **2.** $\frac{1}{7} + \frac{3}{21}$ _____ **3.** $\frac{2}{3} + \frac{1}{5}$ _____

4. $\frac{1}{4} + \frac{2}{3}$ _____ **5.** $\frac{1}{12} + \frac{4}{6}$ _____ **6.** $\frac{1}{2} + \frac{2}{5}$ _____

7. $\frac{1}{6} + \frac{5}{12}$ _____ **8.** $\frac{4}{6} + \frac{1}{3}$ _____ **9.** $\frac{1}{5} + \frac{1}{8}$ _____

10. $\frac{3}{4} + \frac{1}{9}$ _____ **11.** $\frac{6}{12} + \frac{1}{3}$ _____ **12.** $\frac{4}{8} + \frac{1}{2}$ _____

Jeremy collected nickels for one week. He is making stacks of his nickels to determine how many he has. The thickness of one nickel is $\frac{1}{16}$ inch.

13. How tall is a stack of 16 nickels?

_____

14. What is the combined height of 3 nickels, 2 nickels, and 1 nickel?

_____

15. What is the sum of $\frac{5}{30} + \frac{4}{6}$?

A $\frac{5}{6}$ **B** $\frac{7}{9}$ **C** $\frac{2}{3}$ **D** $\frac{9}{12}$

16. How do you rename $\frac{2}{5}$ so you can add it to $\frac{11}{25}$? What is the sum?

_____

_____

_____

Subtracting Fractions with Unlike Denominators

You can subtract fractions with unlike denominators by using the least common multiple (LCM) and the least common denominator (LCD).

Beth wants to exercise for $\frac{4}{5}$ hour. So far, she has exercised for $\frac{2}{3}$ hour. What fraction of an hour does she have left to go?

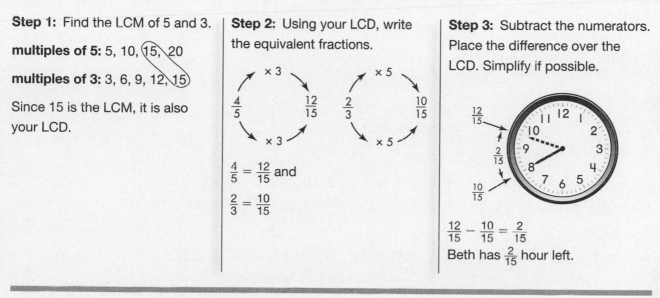

Step 1: Find the LCM of 5 and 3.

multiples of 5: 5, 10, (15,) 20

multiples of 3: 3, 6, 9, 12, 15)

Since 15 is the LCM, it is also your LCD.

Step 2: Using your LCD, write the equivalent fractions.

$\frac{4}{5} = \frac{12}{15}$ and

$\frac{2}{3} = \frac{10}{15}$

Step 3: Subtract the numerators. Place the difference over the LCD. Simplify if possible.

$\frac{12}{15} - \frac{10}{15} = \frac{2}{15}$

Beth has $\frac{2}{15}$ hour left.

In **1** through **7**, find each difference. Simplify if possible.

1. $\frac{3}{4}$
   $-\frac{2}{5}$

2. $\frac{7}{10}$
   $-\frac{1}{5}$

3. $\frac{8}{8}$
   $-\frac{4}{9}$

4. $\frac{17}{18}$
   $-\frac{2}{3}$

5. $\frac{7}{12} - \frac{1}{4} = $ ____

6. $\frac{5}{6} - \frac{3}{8} = $ ____

7. $\frac{23}{24} - \frac{7}{8} = $ ____

8. Natasha had $\frac{7}{8}$ gallon of paint. Her brother Ivan took $\frac{1}{4}$ gallon to paint his model boat. Natasha needs at least $\frac{1}{2}$ gallon to paint her bookshelf. Did Ivan leave her enough paint?

Name _____

Subtracting Fractions with Unlike Denominators

Find the difference. Simplify if necessary.

1. $\frac{10}{12} - \frac{1}{4}$ _____

2. $\frac{9}{10} - \frac{3}{5}$ _____

3. $\frac{7}{8} - \frac{2}{6}$ _____

4. $\frac{7}{12} - \frac{1}{4}$ _____

5. $\frac{4}{5} - \frac{1}{3}$ _____

6. $\frac{2}{3} - \frac{1}{6}$ _____

7. $\frac{4}{8} - \frac{1}{4}$ _____

8. $\frac{4}{10} - \frac{1}{5}$ _____

9. $\frac{9}{9} - \frac{2}{3}$ _____

10. $\frac{9}{15} - \frac{1}{3}$ _____

11. $\frac{4}{12} - \frac{1}{6}$ _____

12. $\frac{14}{20} - \frac{3}{5}$ _____

13. The pet shop owner told Jean to fill her new fish tank $\frac{3}{4}$ full with water. Jean filled it $\frac{9}{12}$ full. What fraction of the tank does Jean still need to fill? _____

14. Paul's dad made a turkey potpie for dinner on Wednesday. The family ate $\frac{4}{8}$ of the pie. On Thursday after school, Paul ate $\frac{2}{16}$ of the pie for a snack. What fraction of the pie remained? _____

15. Gracie read 150 pages of a book. The book is 227 pages long. Which equation shows the amount she still needs to read to finish the story?

A $150 - n = 227$

C $n - 150 = 227$

B $227 + 150 = n$

D $n + 150 = 227$

16. Why do fractions need to have a common denominator before you add or subtract them?

_____

_____

_____

_____

More Adding and Subtracting Fractions

Use what you know about adding and subtracting fractions to solve problems.

Carla wants to make a Veggie Toss using eggplant, green peppers, spring onions, and mushrooms. Besides the eggplant, how many pounds of the other ingredients does she need in all?

Use data from the recipe.

Step 1: Find the amount of green peppers and spring onions. $\frac{1}{3}$ and $\frac{1}{4}$

Step 2: To add these amounts, find a common denominator for both fractions and rewrite each fraction with that denominator.

$$\frac{1}{3} + \frac{1}{4} = \frac{4}{12} + \frac{3}{12} = \frac{7}{12}$$

Step 3: Add the amount of mushrooms to the sum from Step 2. Remember to rewrite the addends with a common denominator.

$$\frac{7}{12} + \frac{3}{8} = \frac{14}{24} + \frac{9}{24} = \frac{23}{24}$$

Carla needs $\frac{23}{24}$ pound of the other veggies in all.

Veggie Toss Recipe	
Eggplant	$\frac{3}{4}$ pound (lb)
Green peppers	$\frac{1}{3}$ pound (lb)
Spring onions	$\frac{1}{4}$ pound (lb)
Mushrooms	$\frac{3}{8}$ pound (lb)

Chop all ingredients to desired size. Toss eggplant with spring onions in olive oil. Add green peppers and saute for 5 minutes. Add mushrooms. Stir. Cover. Simmer over medium low heat until cooked.

For **1** through **3**, use the Veggie Toss Recipe.

1. Suppose you wanted to make a Veggie Toss using spring onions and mushrooms. How many pounds of ingredients do you need? _____

2. How much more eggplant than mushrooms does the recipe call for? _____

3. How much more eggplant does the recipe call for than green peppers and spring onions combined? Show your work.

_____

_____

Name _____

More Adding and Subtracting Fractions

In **1** through **12**, simplify each expression.

1. $\frac{4}{6} + \frac{2}{9}$ _____

2. $\frac{2}{7} + \frac{1}{2}$ _____

3. $\frac{8}{12} + \frac{1}{6}$ _____

4. $\frac{3}{8} + \frac{1}{6}$ _____

5. $\frac{1}{12} + \frac{7}{9}$ _____

6. $\frac{4}{18} + \frac{2}{9}$ _____

7. $\frac{1}{3} + \frac{1}{4}$ _____

8. $\frac{5}{15} + \frac{3}{5}$ _____

9. $\frac{1}{2} - \left(\frac{1}{8} + \frac{1}{8}\right)$ _____

10. $\frac{3}{4} + \left(\frac{1}{4} - \frac{1}{6}\right)$ _____

11. $\left(\frac{1}{2} + \frac{3}{20}\right) - \frac{2}{20}$ _____

12. $\left(\frac{2}{5} + \frac{1}{5}\right) - \frac{3}{10}$ _____

13. A plumber is fitting a water pipe that is $\frac{3}{4}$ foot long on to a water pipe that is $\frac{2}{12}$ foot long. How long will the finished pipe be?

A $\frac{11}{12}$ foot

C $\frac{2}{12}$ foot

B $\frac{8}{16}$ foot

D 1 foot

14. Joel made some muffins. He gave $\frac{1}{4}$ of the muffins to a neighbor. He took $\frac{3}{8}$ of the muffins to school. What fraction of the muffins is left?

A $\frac{4}{12}$

C $\frac{5}{12}$

B $\frac{3}{8}$

D $\frac{8}{8}$

15. Carl has three lengths of cable, $\frac{5}{6}$ yard long, $\frac{1}{4}$ yard long, and $\frac{2}{3}$ yard long. He needs at least 1 yard of cable.

a Which two pieces together make a length at least 1 yard and closest to 1 yard? _____

b If Carl uses the two shortest pieces, how much more cable would he need?

_____

c After Carl has used 1 yard of cable, how much cable will he have left? Explain how you found your answer.

_____

_____

_____

Problem Solving: Draw a Picture and Write an Equation

Read and Understand   Pippa filled $\frac{1}{8}$ of a jar with blue stones, $\frac{1}{4}$ of the jar with yellow stones, and $\frac{1}{2}$ of the jar with purple stones. How much of the jar is filled in all?

What do I know?   Pippa filled $\frac{1}{8}$, $\frac{1}{4}$, and $\frac{1}{2}$ of a jar.

What am I asked to find?   How much of the jar is filled with stones?

Plan   Draw a picture and write an equation.

$$\frac{1}{8} + \frac{1}{4} + \frac{1}{2} = x$$

Solve   Find equal fractions and add. Simplify if you need to.

$$\frac{1}{8} + \frac{1}{4} + \frac{1}{2} = \frac{1}{8} + \frac{2}{8} + \frac{4}{8} = \frac{7}{8}$$

$$x = \frac{7}{8}$$

Pippa filled the jar $\frac{7}{8}$ full of stones.

Draw a picture and write an equation to solve.

1. Joel walked $\frac{2}{5}$ of a mile to the store, $\frac{3}{10}$ of a mile to the library, and $\frac{1}{20}$ of a mile to the post office. Let x = the total distance Joel walked. How far did he walk?

   _____

2. Midge walked $\frac{7}{8}$ mile Monday and $\frac{4}{5}$ mile Tuesday. Let x = how much farther she walked on Monday. How much farther did Midge walk on Monday?

   _____

3. Glenda wrote $\frac{1}{7}$ of her paper on Monday, $\frac{1}{14}$ of her paper on Tuesday, and $\frac{2}{28}$ of her paper on Wednesday. She said she wrote more than half of her paper. Is she correct? Why or why not?

   _____

   _____

R 9·10

Problem Solving: Draw a Picture and Write an Equation

Draw a picture and write an equation to solve.

1. Jamie bought $\frac{5}{8}$ pound of wheat flour. He also bought $\frac{1}{4}$ pound of white flour. How much flour did he buy?

2. Katie is $\frac{3}{5}$ of the way to Brianna's house. Larry is $\frac{7}{10}$ of the way to Brianna's house. How much closer to Brianna's house is Larry?

3. Nina practiced the trumpet for $\frac{1}{6}$ hour. Santiago practiced the trumpet for $\frac{2}{3}$ hour. How much longer did Santiago practice than Nina?

4. Ned caught $\frac{1}{3}$ pound of fish. Sarah caught $\frac{5}{12}$ pound of fish. Jessa caught $\frac{1}{6}$ pound of fish. Which bar diagram shows how to find how many pounds of fish they caught in all?

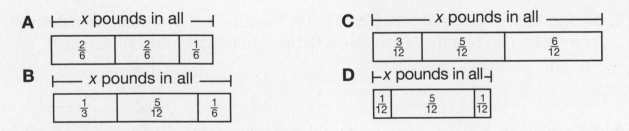

A x pounds in all
| $\frac{2}{6}$ | $\frac{2}{6}$ | $\frac{1}{6}$ |

C x pounds in all
| $\frac{3}{12}$ | $\frac{5}{12}$ | $\frac{6}{12}$ |

B x pounds in all
| $\frac{1}{3}$ | $\frac{5}{12}$ | $\frac{1}{6}$ |

D x pounds in all
| $\frac{1}{12}$ | $\frac{5}{12}$ | $\frac{1}{12}$ |

5. In solving a fraction equation, John added the numerators of several fractions with unlike denominators. What should John have done first?

_____

_____

Improper Fractions and Mixed Numbers

A mixed number combines a whole number with a fraction. It is greater than one.

An improper fraction has a numerator that is larger than its denominator.

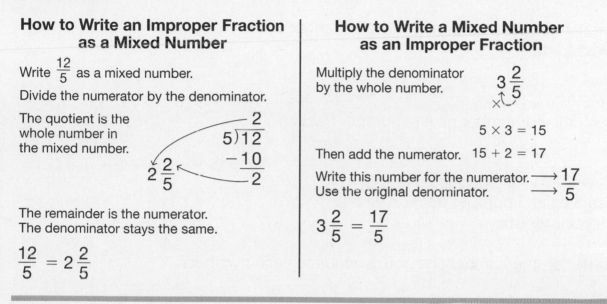

How to Write an Improper Fraction as a Mixed Number

Write $\frac{12}{5}$ as a mixed number.

Divide the numerator by the denominator.

The quotient is the whole number in the mixed number.

$$2\frac{2}{5}$$

$$\begin{array}{r} 2 \\ 5\overline{)12} \\ -10 \\ \hline 2 \end{array}$$

The remainder is the numerator. The denominator stays the same.

$$\frac{12}{5} = 2\frac{2}{5}$$

How to Write a Mixed Number as an Improper Fraction

Multiply the denominator by the whole number. $\quad 3\frac{2}{5}$

$$5 \times 3 = 15$$

Then add the numerator. $15 + 2 = 17$

Write this number for the numerator. ⟶ $\frac{17}{5}$
Use the original denominator.

$$3\frac{2}{5} = \frac{17}{5}$$

1. Draw a picture to show $4\frac{2}{3}$.

For **2–4,** write each improper fraction as a whole number or mixed number in simplest form.

2. $\frac{30}{20}$ _____

3. $\frac{66}{20}$ _____

4. $\frac{24}{14}$ _____

Write each mixed number as an improper fraction.

5. $4\frac{1}{3}$ _____

6. $1\frac{20}{50}$ _____

7. $8\frac{7}{8}$ _____

8. Write 6 as an improper fraction with a denominator of 10. _____

Improper Fractions and Mixed Numbers

1. Draw a picture to show $\frac{8}{6}$.

2. Draw a picture to show $3\frac{5}{6}$.

Write each improper fraction as a whole number or mixed number in simplest form.

3. $\frac{30}{6}$ _____

4. $\frac{47}{9}$ _____

5. $\frac{52}{7}$ _____

Write each mixed number as an improper fraction.

6. $4\frac{4}{5}$ _____

7. $13\frac{3}{4}$ _____

8. $9\frac{5}{8}$ _____

9. Write 8 as an improper fraction with a denominator of 4.

_____

Which letter on the number line corresponds to each number?

```
        F        A C       B      D   E
  <--+--+--+--+--+--+--+--+--+--+--+--+--+--+--+--+-->
    4                  5                  6
```

10. $\frac{27}{5}$ _____

11. $4\frac{7}{10}$ _____

12. $4\frac{3}{5}$ _____

13. Which number does the model represent?

A $\frac{12}{8}$

B $2\frac{3}{8}$

C $2\frac{4}{7}$

D $\frac{20}{8}$

14. Can you express $\frac{9}{9}$ as a mixed number? Why or why not?

_____

_____

P 10·1

Estimating Sums and Differences of Mixed Numbers

You can use rounding to estimate sums and differences of fractions and mixed numbers.

How to round fractions:

If the fractional part is greater than or equal to $\frac{1}{2}$, round up to the next whole number.

Example: Round $3\frac{5}{7}$ to the nearest whole number.

$\frac{5}{7}$ is greater than $\frac{1}{2}$, so $3\frac{5}{7}$ rounds up to 4.

If the fractional part is less than $\frac{1}{2}$, drop the fraction and use the whole number you already have.

Example: Round $6\frac{1}{3}$ to the nearest whole number.

$\frac{1}{3}$ is less than $\frac{1}{2}$, so drop $\frac{1}{3}$ and round down to 6.

How to estimate sums and differences of fractions and mixed numbers:

Round both numbers to the nearest whole number. Then add or subtract.

Example: Estimate $4\frac{1}{8} + 7\frac{2}{3}$.

$4\frac{1}{8}$ rounds down to 4.

$7\frac{2}{3}$ rounds up to 8.

$4 + 8 = 12$

So, $4\frac{1}{8} + 7\frac{2}{3}$ is about 12.

Round to the nearest whole number.

1. $8\frac{5}{6}$ _____   **2.** $13\frac{8}{9}$ _____   **3.** $43\frac{1}{3}$ _____

4. $7\frac{40}{81}$ _____   **5.** $29\frac{4}{5}$ _____   **6.** $88\frac{2}{4}$ _____

7. $19\frac{3}{34}$ _____   **8.** $63\frac{41}{49}$ _____

Estimate each sum or difference.

9. $7\frac{1}{9} + 8\frac{2}{5}$ _____   **10.** $14\frac{5}{8} - 3\frac{7}{10}$ _____

11. $2\frac{1}{4} + 5\frac{1}{2} + 10\frac{3}{4}$ _____   **12.** $11\frac{3}{5} - 4\frac{1}{12}$ _____

13. $9 + 3\frac{11}{14} + 5\frac{1}{9}$ _____   **14.** $15\frac{6}{7} - 12\frac{2}{10}$ _____

Name _____

Estimating Sums and Differences of Mixed Numbers

Round to the nearest whole number.

1. $3\frac{3}{8}$ _____

2. $6\frac{5}{11}$ _____

3. $1\frac{11}{20}$ _____

4. $12\frac{6}{13}$ _____

Estimate each sum or difference.

5. $3\frac{1}{4} + 2\frac{5}{6}$ _____

6. $5\frac{6}{9} - 1\frac{3}{4}$ _____

7. $5\frac{5}{13} + 8\frac{3}{5}$ _____

8. $11 - 6\frac{3}{7} + 2\frac{2}{5}$ _____

Robert and May are competing in a track meet. The table at the right shows the results of their events.

9. Robert says his better jump was about 1 ft longer than May's better jump. Is he correct?

_____

_____

Participant	Event	Results/Distance
Robert	Long jump	**1.** $6\frac{5}{12}$ ft **2.** $5\frac{2}{3}$ ft
	Softball throw	$62\frac{1}{5}$ ft
May	Long jump	**1.** $4\frac{2}{3}$ ft **2.** $4\frac{3}{4}$ ft
	Softball throw	$71\frac{7}{8}$ ft

10. Use the table above. If the school record for the softball throw is 78 ft, about how much farther must Robert throw the ball to match the record?

A 15 ft   **B** 16 ft   **C** 18 ft   **D** 20 ft

11. Consider the sum of $\frac{3}{5} + \frac{3}{4}$. Round each fraction and estimate the sum. Add the two fractions using a common denominator and then round the result. Which estimate is closer to the actual answer?

_____

_____

_____

_____

Modeling Addition and Subtraction of Mixed Numbers

Example 1: Draw a model to add $1\frac{7}{8} + 2\frac{3}{8}$.

Step 1 Model each mixed number using fraction strips.

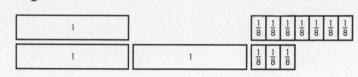

Step 2 Add the fractions. Regroup if you can.

$$\frac{7}{8}$$
$$+\frac{3}{8}$$
$$\frac{10}{8}=1\frac{2}{8}$$

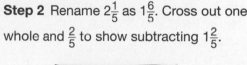

Step 3 Add the whole numbers to the regrouped fractions. Write the sum. Simplify, if possible.

So, $1\frac{7}{8} + 2\frac{3}{8} = 4\frac{1}{4}$.

Example 2: Draw a model to subtract $2\frac{1}{5} - 1\frac{2}{5}$.

Step 1 Model the number you are subtracting from, $2\frac{1}{5}$.

Step 2 Rename $2\frac{1}{5}$ as $1\frac{6}{5}$. Cross out one whole and $\frac{2}{5}$ to show subtracting $1\frac{2}{5}$.

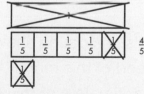

Express the part of the model that is not crossed out as a fraction or mixed number. So, $2\frac{1}{5} - 1\frac{2}{5} = \frac{4}{5}$.

Use fraction strips to find each sum or difference. Simplify, if possible.

1. $3\frac{1}{2} + 1\frac{1}{2}$ **2.** $2\frac{5}{8} + 4\frac{3}{8}$ **3.** $5\frac{2}{6} + 3\frac{5}{6}$ **4.** $2\frac{2}{4} + 6\frac{3}{4}$

5. $6\frac{1}{8} - 3\frac{5}{8}$ **6.** $8\frac{3}{12} - 2\frac{5}{12}$ **7.** $12\frac{1}{3} - 5\frac{2}{3}$ **8.** $9\frac{7}{10} - 6\frac{9}{10}$

Modeling Addition and Subtraction of Mixed Numbers

For **1** and **2**, use each model to find each sum or difference.

1. $1\frac{3}{8} + 1\frac{7}{8}$

2. $3\frac{1}{5} - 1\frac{4}{5}$

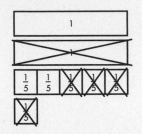

Use fraction strips to find each sum or difference.
Simplify, if possible.

3. $2\frac{1}{3} + 1\frac{2}{3}$ **4.** $3\frac{5}{6} + 4\frac{3}{6}$ **5.** $5\frac{1}{4} - 1\frac{2}{4}$ **6.** $12\frac{3}{8} - 2\frac{5}{8}$

7. $8\frac{1}{6} - 3\frac{5}{6}$ **8.** $4\frac{6}{10} + 5\frac{7}{10}$ **9.** $7\frac{1}{9} - 4\frac{2}{9}$ **10.** $6\frac{2}{5} + 3\frac{4}{5}$

11. $1\frac{1}{6} + 3\frac{5}{6}$ **12.** $2\frac{4}{9} + 6\frac{7}{9}$ **13.** $6\frac{3}{5} - 4\frac{3}{5}$ **14.** $5\frac{1}{3} - 4\frac{2}{3}$

15. Jerome's rain gauge showed $13\frac{9}{10}$ centimeters (cm) at the end of last month. At the end of this month, the rain gauge showed $15\frac{3}{10}$ centimeters. How many more centimeters of rain fell this month?

A $29\frac{2}{10}$ cm   **B** $15\frac{3}{10}$ cm   **C** $2\frac{4}{10}$ cm   **D** $1\frac{4}{10}$ cm

16. You are adding $3\frac{2}{3} + 2\frac{2}{3}$ using fraction strips. Explain how you rename the fraction part of the problem.

_____

_____

Adding Mixed Numbers

Randy talks on the telephone for $2\frac{5}{6}$ hours, and then surfs the Internet for $3\frac{3}{4}$ hours. How many hours does he spend on the two activities?

Step 1. Write equivalent fractions with the least common denominator. You can use fraction strips to show the equivalent fractions.

$$3\frac{3}{4} = 3\frac{9}{12}$$

| 1 | 1 | 1 | ▥▥▥▥ |

$$2\frac{5}{6} = 2\frac{10}{12}$$

| 1 | 1 | ▥▥▥ |

Step 2. Add the fraction part of the mixed number first. Then add the whole numbers.

$$\frac{9}{12} + \frac{10}{12} = \frac{19}{12} \qquad 3 + 2 = 5$$

$$\frac{19}{12} + 5 = 5\frac{19}{12}$$

Step 3. Simplify the sum if possible.

$$5\frac{19}{12} = 6\frac{7}{12} \text{ hours}$$

So, $2\frac{5}{6} + 3\frac{3}{4} = 6\frac{7}{12}$.

In **1** through **6**, find each sum. Simplify if possible.

1. $\quad 2\frac{5}{6}$
$\quad + 3\frac{1}{4}$
$\quad \overline{}$

2. $\quad 1\frac{3}{8}$
$\quad + 6\frac{3}{4}$
$\quad \overline{}$

3. $\quad 5\frac{2}{5}$
$\quad + 4\frac{1}{2}$
$\quad \overline{}$

4. $10\frac{1}{3} + \frac{7}{9} =$ _____

5. $3\frac{1}{4} + 6\frac{2}{3} =$ _____

6. $1\frac{5}{7} + 3\frac{1}{2} =$ _____

7. Tirzah wants to put a fence around her garden. She has 22 yards of fence material. Does she have enough to go all the way around the garden?

_____

_____

_____

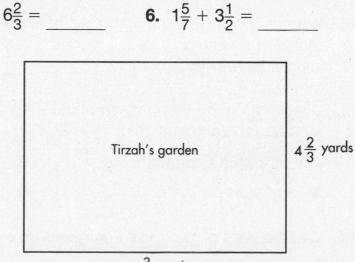

Tirzah's garden $\qquad 4\frac{2}{3}$ yards

$6\frac{3}{4}$ yards

Name _____

Adding Mixed Numbers

In **1** through **6**, find each sum. Simplify, if possible. Estimate for reasonableness.

1. $7\frac{2}{3} + 8\frac{5}{6}$ _____

2. $4\frac{3}{4} + 2\frac{2}{5}$ _____

3. $11\frac{9}{10} + 3\frac{1}{20}$ _____

4. $7\frac{6}{7} + 5\frac{2}{7}$ _____

5. $5\frac{8}{9} + 3\frac{1}{2}$ _____

6. $21\frac{11}{12} + 17\frac{2}{3}$ _____

7. Write two mixed numbers that have a sum of 3.

_____

8. What is the total measure of an average man's brain and heart in kilograms (kg)?

_____

Vital Organ Measures

Average woman's brain	$1\frac{3}{10}$ kg	$2\frac{4}{5}$ lb
Average man's brain	$1\frac{2}{5}$ kg	3 lb
Average human heart	$\frac{3}{10}$ kg	$\frac{7}{10}$ lb

9. What is the total weight of an average woman's brain and heart in pounds (lb)?

_____

10. What is the sum of the measures of an average man's brain and an average woman's brain in kilograms?

_____

11. Which is a good comparison of the estimated sum and the actual sum of $7\frac{7}{8} + 2\frac{11}{12}$?

   A Estimated < actual   **C** Actual > estimated

   B Actual = estimated   **D** Estimated > actual

12. Can the sum of two mixed numbers be equal to 2? Explain why or why not.

_____

_____

_____

Subtracting Mixed Numbers

The Plainville Zoo has had elephants for $12\frac{2}{3}$ years. The zoo has had zebras for $5\frac{1}{2}$ years. How many years longer has the zoo had elephants?

Step 1: Write equivalent fractions with the least common denominator. You can use fraction strips.

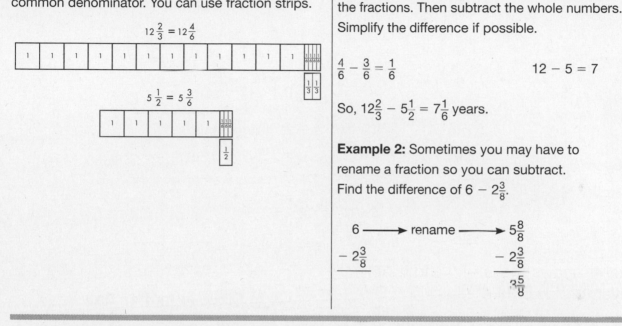

Step 2: Find the difference of $12\frac{4}{6} - 5\frac{3}{6}$. Subtract the fractions. Then subtract the whole numbers. Simplify the difference if possible.

$$\frac{4}{6} - \frac{3}{6} = \frac{1}{6} \qquad\qquad 12 - 5 = 7$$

So, $12\frac{2}{3} - 5\frac{1}{2} = 7\frac{1}{6}$ years.

Example 2: Sometimes you may have to rename a fraction so you can subtract. Find the difference of $6 - 2\frac{3}{8}$.

$$
\begin{array}{ccc}
6 & \longrightarrow \text{rename} \longrightarrow & 5\frac{8}{8} \\
-\,2\frac{3}{8} & & -\,2\frac{3}{8} \\
\hline
& & 3\frac{5}{8}
\end{array}
$$

For **1** through **4**, find each difference. Simplify, if possible.
Remember: You may have to rename a fraction in order to subtract.

1. $\quad 4\frac{3}{5}$
   $\quad -2\frac{1}{3}$

2. $\quad 5\frac{6}{7}$
   $\quad -1\frac{1}{2}$

3. $\quad 3$
   $\quad -1\frac{3}{4}$

4. $\quad 6\frac{5}{6}$
   $\quad -5\frac{1}{2}$

5. To find the difference of $7 - 3\frac{5}{12}$, how do you rename the 7?

_____

6. Robyn ran $5\frac{3}{4}$ miles last week. She ran $4\frac{1}{10}$ miles this week. How many more miles did she run last week?

_____

Name _____

Subtracting Mixed Numbers

For **1** through **10**, find each difference. Simplify, if possible.

1. $10\frac{3}{4}$
    $-\ 7\frac{1}{4}$
    _____

2. $7\frac{3}{7}$
    $-\ 2\frac{8}{21}$
    _____

3. 3
    $-\ 2\frac{2}{3}$
    _____

4. $17\frac{7}{8}$
    $-\ 12\frac{3}{12}$
    _____

5. $9\frac{5}{9} - 6\frac{5}{6}$ _____

6. $4\frac{3}{4} - 2\frac{2}{3}$ _____

7. $6\frac{1}{4} - 3\frac{1}{3}$ _____

8. $5\frac{1}{5} - 3\frac{7}{8}$ _____

9. $8\frac{2}{7} - 7\frac{1}{3}$ _____

10. $2\frac{9}{10} - 2\frac{1}{3}$ _____

The table shows the length and width of several kinds of bird eggs.

11. How much longer is the Canada goose egg than the raven egg?

_____

12. How much wider is the turtledove egg than the robin egg?

_____

Egg Sizes in Inches (in.)

Bird	Length	Width
Canada goose	$3\frac{2}{5}$	$2\frac{3}{10}$
Robin	$\frac{3}{4}$	$\frac{3}{5}$
Turtledove	$1\frac{1}{5}$	$\frac{9}{10}$
Raven	$1\frac{9}{10}$	$1\frac{3}{10}$

13. Which is the difference of $21\frac{15}{16} - 18\frac{3}{4}$?

   A $2\frac{7}{16}$ **B** $2\frac{9}{16}$ **C** $3\frac{3}{16}$ **D** $3\frac{9}{16}$

14. Explain why it is necessary to rename $4\frac{1}{4}$ if you subtract $\frac{3}{4}$ from it.

_____

_____

_____

More Adding and Subtracting Mixed Numbers

You can use what you know about adding and subtracting with mixed numbers when you simplify expressions with mixed numbers.

Simplify $\left(4\frac{1}{8} + 6\frac{1}{4}\right) - 2\frac{1}{2}$.

Step 1 Add the mixed numbers in parentheses first. Find a common denominator.

$$4\frac{1}{8} + 6\frac{1}{4}$$
$$\downarrow \qquad \downarrow$$
$$4\frac{1}{8} + 6\frac{2}{8} = 10\frac{3}{8}$$

Step 2 Subtract $2\frac{1}{2}$ from the sum you found. Find a common denominator.

$$10\frac{3}{8} - 2\frac{1}{2}$$
$$\downarrow \qquad \downarrow$$
$$10\frac{3}{8} - 2\frac{4}{8} \qquad \text{You can't subtract } \frac{4}{8} \text{ from } \frac{3}{8}.$$

Step 3 Rename if possible.

$$9\frac{11}{8} - 2\frac{4}{8} = 7\frac{7}{8}$$

In **1** through **9**, simplify each expression. Remember to rename mixed numbers if possible.

1. $\left(12\frac{4}{7} + 2\frac{3}{14}\right) - 2\frac{6}{14}$

2. $\left(5\frac{1}{2} + 2\frac{3}{4}\right) - 3\frac{1}{2}$

3. $10\frac{5}{16} - \left(5\frac{1}{4} + 2\frac{9}{16}\right)$

4. $\frac{6}{9} + \frac{5}{18} + 1\frac{3}{6}$

5. $1\frac{4}{10} + 1\frac{3}{20} + 1\frac{1}{5}$

6. $\left(3\frac{3}{8} - 1\frac{1}{5}\right) + 1\frac{7}{8}$

7. $1\frac{2}{12} + \frac{1}{6} + 7\frac{3}{4}$

8. $\left(1\frac{5}{8} + 3\frac{1}{4}\right) - 1\frac{20}{24}$

9. $5\frac{1}{4} + 7\frac{3}{20} + 1\frac{3}{4}$

10. Suzy spent $6\frac{7}{8}$ days working on her English paper, $3\frac{1}{6}$ days doing her science project, and $1\frac{1}{2}$ days studying for her math test. How many days more did Suzy spend on her English paper and math test than on her science project?

Name _____

More Adding and Subtracting Mixed Numbers

In **1** through **16**, simplify each expression.

1. $2\frac{1}{8} + 4\frac{2}{3}$

2. $9\frac{1}{6} - 3\frac{2}{9}$

3. $8\frac{1}{4} - 6\frac{5}{8}$

4. $6\frac{4}{5} + 5\frac{3}{10}$

5. $\left(3\frac{1}{2} + 8\frac{2}{3}\right) - 3\frac{5}{6}$

6. $\left(14\frac{1}{6} - 4\frac{5}{9}\right) + 1\frac{7}{18}$

7. $7\frac{7}{12} + \left(3\frac{1}{2} + 1\frac{7}{8}\right)$

8. $\left(10\frac{1}{4} - 5\frac{5}{8}\right) - 1\frac{3}{8}$

9. $100\frac{3}{10} - 60\frac{2}{3} - 5\frac{2}{15}$

10. $25\frac{3}{8} - \left(10\frac{4}{5} + 5\frac{7}{8}\right)$

11. $\left(2\frac{2}{3} + 4\frac{5}{6}\right) + 3\frac{3}{8}$

12. $\left(30\frac{1}{9} + 4\frac{1}{3}\right) - 19\frac{5}{6}$

13. $7\frac{2}{3} + \left(5\frac{1}{6} - 1\frac{5}{9}\right)$

14. Which shows three mixed numbers that have sum of 10?

    A $1\frac{2}{3} + 3\frac{5}{12} + 4\frac{3}{4}$

    C $2\frac{3}{8} + 5\frac{1}{2} + 1\frac{1}{4}$

    B $3\frac{1}{3} + 3\frac{1}{4} + 3\frac{5}{12}$

    D $5\frac{1}{4} + 1\frac{7}{8} + 3\frac{7}{8}$

15. What is a reasonable estimate for the sum of $4\frac{1}{8} + 3\frac{2}{3} + 5\frac{1}{2}$?

_____

16. Veronica is buying cubed cheese from Mr. Sand's deli. She asks for $1\frac{3}{4}$ pounds. When Mr. Sand places some cheese in a container and weighs it, the scale shows $1\frac{1}{4}$ pounds. The container weighs $\frac{1}{16}$ pound. How many more pounds of cheese would Mr. Sand need to add to the scale to get the amount that Veronica asked for? Explain how you solved the problem.

_____

_____

_____

_____

_____

Problem Solving: Draw a Picture and Write an Equation

A jeweler has a strand of gold wire that is $1\frac{3}{8}$ inches. He cuts $\frac{3}{4}$ of an inch of wire to make a loop. How long is the remaining piece of wire?

Read and Understand

What do you know?

The length of the wire is $1\frac{3}{8}$ inches.

The length he cuts off is $\frac{3}{4}$ of an inch.

What are you trying to find?

The length of the wire that is left over.

Plan and Solve

Draw a picture for what you know.

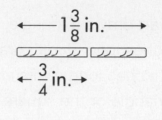

Write an equation.
Let x = the length of wire left over.

$1\frac{3}{8} - \frac{3}{4} = x$

Solve the problem.

$1\frac{3}{8} - \frac{6}{8} = \frac{11}{8} - \frac{6}{8} = \frac{5}{8}$

Write the answer in a sentence.

The remaining wire is $\frac{5}{8}$ inch long.

Look Back and Check

Is your answer correct?

Yes, $\frac{3}{4} + \frac{5}{8} = \frac{6}{8} + \frac{5}{8} = \frac{11}{8} = 1\frac{3}{8}$

From his house, Jason rode his bike $1\frac{1}{3}$ miles to the post office.
He then rode in the same direction to the park, which is $\frac{1}{4}$ of a mile from the post office. How far did Jason ride?

1. To the right, draw a picture to represent the problem to be solved. Let x = the distance Jason rode from his house to the park.

   _____

2. Write an equation that represents this distance. Then solve for x. _____

Problem Solving: Draw a Picture and Write an Equation

Draw a picture and write an equation. Then solve.

1. Mr. Flanders drives $1\frac{2}{3}$ miles to school and $1\frac{2}{3}$ miles home each day. He also drives an extra $2\frac{2}{7}$ miles to go to the gym. How many miles does he drive in one day?

_____

_____

2. Alison is making a 16-inch necklace. The first $4\frac{1}{4}$ inches are filled with red beads and $8\frac{3}{8}$ inches are filled with blue beads. The rest has white beads. How many inches are filled with white beads?

_____

3. Stewart draws a triangle, and each side is $2\frac{1}{6}$ inches long. Judith draws a square, and each side is $1\frac{5}{8}$ inches long. Which figure has the greater perimeter, the triangle or the square?

_____

_____

4. Cristoff practices playing his guitar for $1\frac{1}{2}$ hours each weekday. He practices this amount of time plus an additional $1\frac{1}{2}$ hours on Sundays. Let $x =$ the number of hours Cristoff practices on Sundays. Draw a picture and write an equation and solve to find the number of hours he practices on Sundays.

_____

5. Which of these fractions, when added to $2\frac{1}{3}$, will give you a sum greater than six?

A $3\frac{1}{2}$ B $3\frac{5}{12}$ C $3\frac{7}{12}$ D $3\frac{3}{4}$

6. Dennis says that $1\frac{1}{2}$, $1\frac{2}{4}$, and $1\frac{3}{6}$ are all equivalent. Is he correct? Draw a picture and explain your answer.

_____

_____

Fractions and Division

You can think of fractions as division: The numerator is the same
as the dividend and the denominator is the same as the divisor.

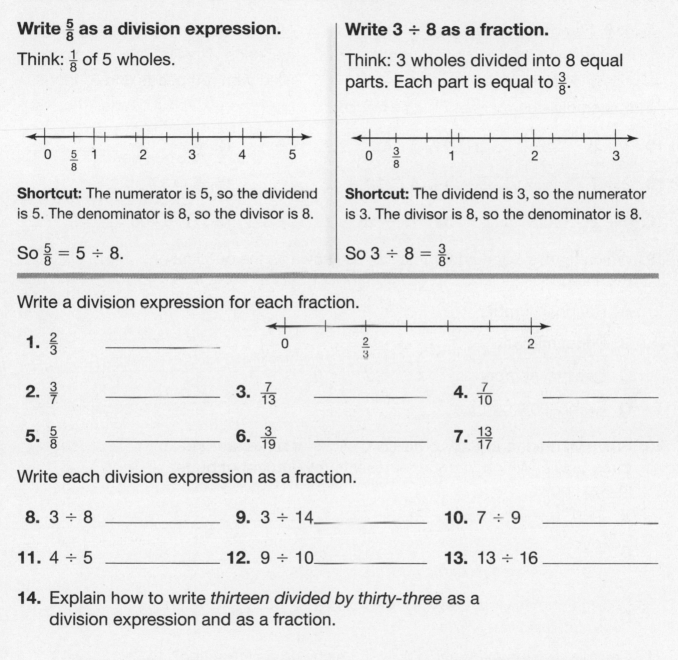

Write $\frac{5}{8}$ as a division expression.

Think: $\frac{1}{8}$ of 5 wholes.

Shortcut: The numerator is 5, so the dividend
is 5. The denominator is 8, so the divisor is 8.

So $\frac{5}{8} = 5 \div 8$.

Write 3 ÷ 8 as a fraction.

Think: 3 wholes divided into 8 equal
parts. Each part is equal to $\frac{3}{8}$.

Shortcut: The dividend is 3, so the numerator
is 3. The divisor is 8, so the denominator is 8.

So $3 \div 8 = \frac{3}{8}$.

Write a division expression for each fraction.

1. $\frac{2}{3}$ _____

2. $\frac{3}{7}$ _____ **3.** $\frac{7}{13}$ _____ **4.** $\frac{7}{10}$ _____

5. $\frac{5}{8}$ _____ **6.** $\frac{3}{19}$ _____ **7.** $\frac{13}{17}$ _____

Write each division expression as a fraction.

8. 3 ÷ 8 _____ **9.** 3 ÷ 14 _____ **10.** 7 ÷ 9 _____

11. 4 ÷ 5 _____ **12.** 9 ÷ 10 _____ **13.** 13 ÷ 16 _____

14. Explain how to write *thirteen divided by thirty-three* as a
division expression and as a fraction.

_____

_____

_____

_____

Fractions and Division

Write a division expression for each fraction.

1. $\frac{2}{9}$ _____

2. $\frac{1}{7}$ _____

3. $\frac{7}{10}$ _____

4. $\frac{3}{4}$ _____

5. $\frac{7}{8}$ _____

6. $\frac{3}{16}$ _____

7. $\frac{6}{13}$ _____

8. $\frac{18}{23}$ _____

9. $\frac{11}{12}$ _____

Write each division expression as a fraction.

10. $3 \div 8$ _____

11. $3 \div 16$ _____

12. $6 \div 11$ _____

13. $2 \div 7$ _____

14. $4 \div 10$ _____

15. $5 \div 17$ _____

16. $4 \div 9$ _____

17. $13 \div 23$ _____

18. $17 \div 100$ _____

19. Which term is any number that can be shown as the quotient of two integers?

   A Rational number

   B Prime number

   C Decimal number

   D Compatible number

20. Steve wanted to equally divide two sticks of butter among three bowls. Which fraction represents the amount of butter in each bowl?

   A $\frac{5}{2}$

   B $\frac{2}{3}$

   C $\frac{3}{2}$

   D $\frac{3}{6}$

21. Can the division expression $4 \div 15$ be shown as a fraction? If yes, write the fraction. Explain why or why not.

   _____

   _____

Multiplying Fractions and Whole Numbers

You can find the product of a fraction and a whole number.

Tran needs $\frac{2}{3}$ yard of fabric to sew a pair of shorts. How many yards of fabric will Tran need to sew 6 pairs of shorts?

Step 1. Multiply the numerator by the whole number.	**Step 2.** Place the product over the denominator. Simplify if possible.
$2 \times 6 = 12$	$\frac{12}{3} = 4$ yards of fabric

Remember: In word problems, "of" means "multiply."

Example: $\frac{3}{5}$ of $15 = \frac{3}{5} \times 15$

In questions **1–4**, find each product. Simplify if possible.

1. $\frac{1}{3} \times 60 =$ _____

2. $\frac{3}{4}$ of $32 =$ _____

3. $\frac{7}{8} \times 40 =$ _____

4. $\frac{2}{7}$ of $35 =$ _____

For questions **5–7**, use the table to the right.

5. What is $\frac{1}{7}$ the speed of a cheetah? _____

6. What is $\frac{1}{5}$ the speed of a cat? _____

7. What is $\frac{1}{5}$ the speed of a jackal? _____

Animal	Speed (in mi/h)
Cat	30
Cheetah	70
Jackal	35

Multiplying Fractions and Whole Numbers

Find each product.

1. $\frac{1}{4}$ of 96 = _____

2. $\frac{4}{7}$ of 28 = _____

3. $\frac{3}{4} \times 72$ = _____

4. $45 \times \frac{3}{9}$ = _____

5. $56 \times \frac{7}{8}$ = _____

6. $42 \times \frac{3}{7}$ = _____

7. $\frac{1}{2}$ of 118 = _____

8. $\frac{3}{8}$ of 56 = _____

9. $\frac{1}{10} \times 400$ = _____

10. $84 \times \frac{1}{6}$ = _____

11. $64 \times \frac{5}{16}$ = _____

12. $40 \times \frac{11}{20}$ = _____

13. $\frac{5}{8}$ of 48 = _____

14. $\frac{1}{7}$ of 77 = _____

15. $\frac{4}{5} \times 90$ = _____

16. $42 \times \frac{3}{14}$ = _____

17. $72 \times \frac{5}{8}$ = _____

18. $18 \times \frac{2}{3}$ = _____

19. $\frac{5}{6} \times 84$ = _____

20. $\frac{11}{12} \times 144$ = _____

21. $\frac{6}{7} \times 42$ = _____

22. Complete the table by writing the product of each expression in the box below it. Use a pattern to find each product. Explain the pattern.

$\frac{1}{2} \times 32$	$\frac{1}{4} \times 32$	$\frac{1}{8} \times 32$	$\frac{1}{16} \times 32$

_____

23. **Reasoning** If $\frac{1}{2}$ of 1 is $\frac{1}{2}$, what is $\frac{1}{2}$ of 2, 3, and 4? _____

24. Which is $\frac{2}{3}$ of 225?

    A 75   **B** 113   **C** 150   **D** 450

25. **Explain It** Explain why $\frac{1}{2}$ of 2 equals one whole.

_____

_____

Name _____

Estimating Products

When you are working with fractions and mixed numbers, you can estimate using rounding, compatible numbers, or compatible benchmark fractions.

Estimate $\frac{3}{10} \times 21$ using a whole number that is compatible with the denominator.

$\frac{3}{10} \times 21$ Change 21 to the nearest whole number that is compatible with 10.

$\downarrow \quad \downarrow$

$\frac{3}{10} \times 20 = 6$

$\frac{3}{10} \times 21 \approx 6$ Think: $20 \div 10 = 2$.

$3 \times 2 = 6$.

Estimate $\frac{3}{10} \times 12$ using a compatible benchmark fraction.

$\frac{3}{10} \times 12$ Round $\frac{3}{10}$ to a compatible benchmark fraction. Since $\frac{3}{10}$ is close to $\frac{1}{4}$ and 4 is a factor of twelve, use $\frac{1}{4}$.

$\downarrow \quad \downarrow$

$\frac{1}{4} \times 12 = 3$

$\frac{3}{10} \times 12 \approx 3$ Think: $12 \div 4 = 3$.

$1 \times 3 = 3$.

Estimate each product by using compatible numbers or benchmark fractions.

1. $\frac{1}{5} \times 20 = $ _____

2. $\frac{4}{7} \times 12 = $ _____

3. $\frac{5}{8} \times 20 = $ _____

4. $31 \times \frac{3}{5} = $ _____

5. $\frac{7}{12} \times 27 = $ _____

6. $\frac{9}{16} \times 70 = $ _____

7. $31 \times \frac{2}{7} = $ _____

8. $24 \times \frac{5}{12} = $ _____

9. $12 \times \frac{4}{9} = $ _____

Estimate each product by rounding each factor to the nearest whole number.

10. $10\frac{2}{3} \times 3\frac{1}{8} \rightarrow$ Round $10\frac{2}{3}$: _____ Round $3\frac{1}{8}$: _____ Multiply: _____

11. $9\frac{2}{9} \times 3\frac{5}{6} = $ _____

12. $5\frac{7}{8} \times 6\frac{3}{4} = $ _____

13. $2\frac{1}{5} \times 6\frac{4}{10} = $ _____

14. Josh used $\frac{3}{7} \times 21$ as a compatible number estimate for $\frac{3}{7} \times 20$. Is his estimate reasonable? Why or why not?

_____

15. Which estimate for $\frac{7}{12} \times 20$ is better than the other?

$\frac{7}{12} \times 20 \approx \frac{7}{12} \times 24 = 14$ $\frac{7}{12} \times 20 \approx \frac{1}{2} \times 20 = 10$.

_____

_____

_____

_____

Name _____

Estimating Products

Estimate each product.

1. $2\frac{3}{8} \times \frac{1}{3}$ _____

2. $6 \times 2\frac{1}{5}$ _____

3. $\frac{6}{10} \times 5\frac{3}{4}$ _____

4. $3\frac{7}{9} \times 6\frac{2}{5}$ _____

5. $2\frac{1}{2} \times 2\frac{1}{3}$ _____

6. $\frac{7}{8} \times 4\frac{3}{8}$ _____

7. $27 \times \frac{3}{8}$ _____

8. $\frac{1}{4} \times 17$ _____

9. $\frac{3}{5} \times 51$ _____

10. $8\frac{4}{9} \times 3\frac{6}{7}$ _____

11. $\frac{12}{15} \times 8$ _____

12. $17 \times \frac{1}{2}$ _____

13. $\frac{1}{3} \times 2\frac{4}{10}$ _____

14. $7\frac{5}{8} \times 2\frac{2}{3}$ _____

15. $\frac{5}{12} \times 12$ _____

16. Show three ways to estimate $\frac{3}{5} \times 9\frac{1}{2}$. Identify each method you use.

_____

_____

17. Jenna lives $4\frac{3}{10}$ miles from school. She estimates that she travels
$4 \times 2 \times 5$, or 40 miles each week. Is her estimate an overestimate
or an underestimate? Explain.

_____

_____

18. Which benchmark fraction could you use to estimate the product of $36 \times \frac{11}{16}$? _____

19. Estimation Which is the best estimate for the area of a square with sides
equal to $4\frac{1}{8}$ inches?

    A 6 sq in.

    B 12 sq in.

    C 16 sq in.

    D 20 sq in.

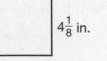

$4\frac{1}{8}$ in.

20. Bryce has 24 baseball trophies. Matt has $\frac{3}{4}$ as many trophies as Bryce.
How many trophies does Matt have?

    A 6 trophies

    B 12 trophies

    C 18 trophies

    D 24 trophies

Multiplying Two Fractions

Musa and Karen are riding a bike path that is $\frac{4}{5}$ mile long. Karen's bike got a flat tire $\frac{3}{10}$ of the way down the path and she had to stop. How many miles did Karen ride?

You can find the product of two fractions by drawing a diagram.

Step 1. Draw a diagram using shading to represent $\frac{4}{5}$.

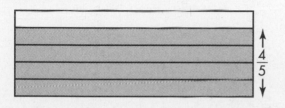

Step 2. Draw lines vertically using dots to represent $\frac{3}{10}$.

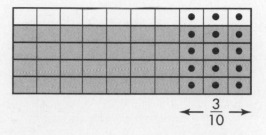

Step 3. Count the parts of the diagram that are shaded and dotted. This is the product numerator.

12

Step 4. Count the total number of parts of the diagram. This is the product denominator.

50

Step 5. Simplify if possible.

$$\frac{12}{50} = \frac{6}{25}$$

Another way to find the product:

Step 1. Multiply the numerators: $4 \times 3 = 12$.

Step 2. Multiply the denominators: $5 \times 10 = 50$.

Step 3. Simplify if possible: $\frac{12}{50} = \frac{6}{25}$.

In **1** through **6**, find the product. Simplify if possible.

1. $\frac{1}{3} \times \frac{2}{5} =$ _____

2. $\frac{5}{8} \times \frac{1}{4} =$ _____

3. $\frac{5}{6} \times \frac{3}{10} =$ _____

4. $\frac{1}{2} \times 6 =$ _____

5. $14 \times \frac{3}{7} =$ _____

6. $\frac{3}{5} \times \frac{1}{2} \times \frac{6}{7} =$ _____

7. Using a diagram, show $\frac{3}{7} \times \frac{1}{4}$.

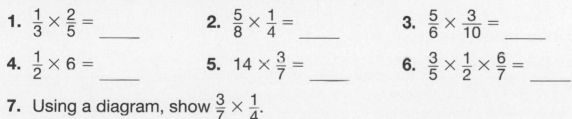

Name _____

Multiplying Two Fractions

Write the multiplication problem that each model represents then solve. Put your answer in simplest form.

1. [grid model]

_____

2. [grid model]

_____

Find each product. Simplify if possible.

3. $\frac{7}{8} \times \frac{4}{5} =$ _____

4. $\frac{3}{7} \times \frac{2}{3} =$ _____

5. $\frac{1}{6} \times \frac{2}{5} =$ _____

6. $\frac{2}{7} \times \frac{1}{4} =$ _____

7. $\frac{2}{9} \times \frac{1}{2} =$ _____

8. $\frac{3}{4} \times \frac{1}{3} =$ _____

9. $\frac{3}{8} \times \frac{4}{9} =$ _____

10. $\frac{1}{5} \times \frac{5}{6} =$ _____

11. $\frac{2}{3} \times \frac{5}{6} \times 14 =$ _____

12. $\frac{1}{2} \times \frac{1}{3} \times \frac{1}{4} =$ _____

13. If $\frac{4}{5} \times \blacksquare = \frac{2}{5}$, what is $\blacksquare$? _____

14. In Mrs. Marshall's classroom, $\frac{6}{7}$ of the students play sports. Of the students who play sports, $\frac{4}{5}$ also play an instrument. If there are 35 students in her class, how many play sports and an instrument?

_____

15. Which does the model represent?

[dot grid model]

A $\frac{3}{8} \times \frac{3}{5}$　　**C** $\frac{3}{5} \times \frac{5}{8}$

B $\frac{7}{8} \times \frac{2}{5}$　　**D** $\frac{4}{8} \times \frac{3}{5}$

16. Describe a model that represents $\frac{3}{3} \times \frac{4}{4}$

_____

_____

Area of a Rectangle

You have learned how to multiply fractions by finding the area of a rectangle.

What is the area of a horse pasture that is $\frac{3}{8}$ mile long by $\frac{2}{3}$ mile wide?

You can draw the pasture on a 24 × 24 grid.

$\frac{3}{8} = \frac{9}{24}$ Change each length and width to 24ths.

$\frac{2}{3} = \frac{16}{24}$

Area = length × width

$\frac{2}{3} \times \frac{3}{8} =$

$\frac{16}{24} \times \frac{9}{24} = \frac{144}{576}$

$\frac{144}{576} = \frac{1}{4}.$

So, the pasture has an area of $\frac{1}{4}$ square mile.

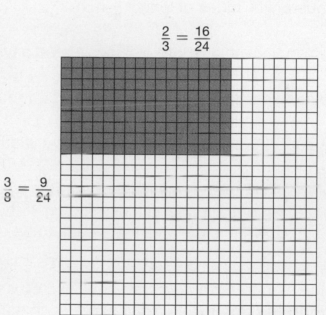

$\frac{2}{3} = \frac{16}{24}$

$\frac{3}{8} = \frac{9}{24}$

For questions 1-2, find each area.

1. a rectangle with sides of lengths $\frac{1}{6}$ yard and $\frac{3}{4}$ yard _____

2. a square with sides of lengths $\frac{2}{5}$ inch _____

3. **Writing to Explain** Is $\frac{5}{8}$ sq. in. a reasonable answer for the area of a rectangle with lengths of $\frac{1}{8}$ inch by 5 inches?

_____

_____

_____

Area of a Rectangle

Find each area.

1. a rectangle with sides of lengths $\frac{4}{5}$ foot and $\frac{1}{2}$ foot   _____

2. a rectangle with sides of lengths $\frac{1}{3}$ yard and $\frac{3}{4}$ yard   _____

3. a rectangle with sides of lengths $\frac{2}{3}$ foot and $\frac{1}{3}$ foot   _____

4. a rectangle with sides of lengths $\frac{5}{6}$ inch and $\frac{1}{3}$ inch   _____

5. a square with sides of length $\frac{5}{8}$ inch   _____

6. a rectangle with a length of 3 inches and a width of $\frac{1}{8}$ inch   _____

7. a rectangle with a length of $\frac{1}{5}$ yard and a width of $\frac{2}{3}$ yard   _____

8. a rectangle with a length of $\frac{4}{9}$ foot and a width of 2 feet   _____

9. Mrs. Henley built a cage for her bird. She wanted to cover the bottom of the cage with newspaper. If the cage is $\frac{1}{4}$ yard by $\frac{1}{2}$ yard, what is the area that needs to be covered?

   A $\frac{1}{8}$ sq. yd   B $\frac{1}{4}$ sq. yd   C $\frac{1}{2}$ sq. yd   D 8 sq. yd

10. **Writing to Explain** Tariq and Marie each multiplied $\frac{1}{8}$ inch × $\frac{5}{8}$ inch. Tariq got $\frac{5}{8}$ sq. in. and Marie got $\frac{5}{64}$ sq. in. Which student found the correct area? How do you know?

    _____

    _____

    _____

Name _____

Multiplying Mixed Numbers

You can find the product of two mixed numbers.

Millwood City is constructing a new highway through town. The construction crew can complete $5\frac{3}{5}$ miles of road each month. How many miles will they complete in $6\frac{1}{2}$ months?

Step 1. Round the mixed numbers to whole numbers so you can make an estimate.

$$5\frac{3}{5} \times 6\frac{1}{2}$$
$$6 \times 7 = 42$$

So, they can complete about 42 miles.

Step 2. Write the mixed numbers as improper fractions.

$$5\frac{3}{5} \times 6\frac{1}{2} = \frac{28}{5} \times \frac{13}{2}$$

Step 3. Multiply the numerators and the denominators. Simplify the product if possible. Remember to look for common factors.

$$\overset{14}{\cancel{28}}{5} \times \frac{13}{\underset{1}{\cancel{2}}} = \frac{182}{5} = 36\frac{2}{5}$$

Step 4. Compare your product to your estimate to check for reasonableness.

$36\frac{2}{5}$ is close to 42, so this answer is reasonable.

The construction crew will complete $36\frac{2}{5}$ miles of highway in $6\frac{1}{2}$ months.

For **1** through **6**, estimate a product. Then solve for each actual product. Simplify if possible.

1. $1\frac{3}{4} \times 2\frac{1}{2} = $ _____

2. $1\frac{1}{5} \times 1\frac{2}{3} = $ _____

3. $2 \times 2\frac{1}{4} = $ _____

4. $1\frac{2}{5} \times 2\frac{1}{4} = $ _____

5. $2\frac{1}{2} \times 10 = $ _____

6. $1\frac{2}{3} \times \frac{1}{5} = $ _____

7. Using the example above, the new highway will be a total of 54 miles long. Will the highway be finished in 8 months?

_____

8. Sayed gave an answer of $6\frac{6}{7}$ for the problem $4\frac{2}{7} \times 1\frac{3}{5}$. Using estimates, is this a reasonable answer?

_____

Name _____

Multiplying Mixed Numbers

Estimate the product. Then complete the multiplication.

1. $5\frac{4}{5} \times 7 = \dfrac{\boxed{}}{5} \times \dfrac{7}{1} = \boxed{}$

2. $3\frac{2}{3} \times 5\frac{1}{7} = \dfrac{\boxed{}}{3} \times \dfrac{\boxed{}}{7} = \boxed{}$

Estimate. Then find each product. Simplify.

3. $4\frac{3}{5} \times \frac{2}{3}$ _____

4. $6 \times 2\frac{2}{7}$ _____

5. $7\frac{4}{5} \times 2\frac{1}{3}$ _____

6. $3\frac{3}{4} \times 2\frac{4}{5}$ _____

7. $2\frac{1}{5} \times \frac{7}{8}$ _____

8. $6\frac{1}{3} \times 1\frac{5}{6}$ _____

9. $1\frac{4}{5} \times 1\frac{1}{3} \times 1\frac{3}{4}$ _____

10. $\frac{3}{4} \times 2\frac{2}{3} \times 5\frac{1}{5}$ _____

11. Write a mixed number for p so that $3\frac{1}{4} \times p$ is more than $3\frac{1}{4}$.

_____

12. A model house is built on a base that measures $9\frac{1}{4}$ in. wide and $8\frac{4}{5}$ in. long. What is the total area of the model house's base?

_____

13. Which is $1\frac{3}{4}$ of $150\frac{1}{2}$?

  A 263   **B** $263\frac{1}{8}$ **C** $263\frac{3}{8}$ **D** $264\frac{3}{8}$

14. Megan's dog Sparky eats $4\frac{1}{4}$ cups of food each day. Explain how Megan can determine how much food to give Sparky if she needs to feed him only $\frac{2}{3}$ as much. Solve the problem.

_____

_____

Multiplication as Scaling

Think of multiplication as scaling or resizing.

Example 1: $2\frac{1}{2} \times 5 > 5$

Multiplying a number by a fraction greater than 1 results in a product greater than the starting number.

Example 2: $\frac{3}{4} \times 5 < 5$

Multiplying a number by a fraction less than 1 results in a product less than the starting number.

Example 3: $\frac{2}{2} \times 5 = 5$

Multiplying by a fraction equal to 1 results in a product equal to the starting number.

Without multiplying, decide which symbol belongs in the box: $<$, $>$, or $=$.

1. $3\frac{1}{2} \times 3\frac{1}{3}$ ☐ $3\frac{1}{2}$

2. $\frac{2}{3} \times 2\frac{1}{3}$ ☐ $2\frac{1}{3}$

3. $8\frac{2}{5} \times \frac{5}{5}$ ☐ $8\frac{2}{5}$

4. $\frac{3}{4} \times 4\frac{2}{3}$ ☐ $4\frac{2}{3}$

5. $4\frac{1}{2} \times 1\frac{1}{3}$ ☐ $1\frac{1}{3}$

6. $\frac{2}{5} \times 5\frac{2}{3}$ ☐ $5\frac{2}{3}$

7. $3\frac{2}{5} \times \frac{4}{4}$ ☐ $3\frac{2}{5}$

8. $\frac{5}{8} \times 8\frac{1}{3}$ ☐ $8\frac{1}{3}$

9. $5\frac{1}{2} \times 6\frac{2}{3}$ ☐ $6\frac{2}{3}$

10. $\frac{3}{8} \times 2\frac{1}{3}$ ☐ $2\frac{1}{3}$

11. $10\frac{2}{5} \times \frac{8}{8}$ ☐ $10\frac{2}{5}$

12. $\frac{1}{2} \times 9\frac{1}{3}$ ☐ $9\frac{1}{3}$

Multiplication as Scaling

In **1-20**, without multiplying, decide which symbol belongs in the box: <, >, or =.

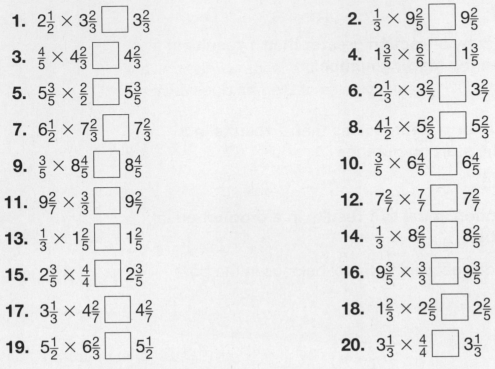

1. $2\frac{1}{2} \times 3\frac{2}{3}$ ☐ $3\frac{2}{3}$

2. $\frac{1}{3} \times 9\frac{2}{5}$ ☐ $9\frac{2}{5}$

3. $\frac{4}{5} \times 4\frac{2}{3}$ ☐ $4\frac{2}{3}$

4. $1\frac{3}{5} \times \frac{6}{6}$ ☐ $1\frac{3}{5}$

5. $5\frac{3}{5} \times \frac{2}{2}$ ☐ $5\frac{3}{5}$

6. $2\frac{1}{3} \times 3\frac{2}{7}$ ☐ $3\frac{2}{7}$

7. $6\frac{1}{2} \times 7\frac{2}{3}$ ☐ $7\frac{2}{3}$

8. $4\frac{1}{2} \times 5\frac{2}{3}$ ☐ $5\frac{2}{3}$

9. $\frac{3}{5} \times 8\frac{4}{5}$ ☐ $8\frac{4}{5}$

10. $\frac{3}{5} \times 6\frac{4}{5}$ ☐ $6\frac{4}{5}$

11. $9\frac{2}{7} \times \frac{3}{3}$ ☐ $9\frac{2}{7}$

12. $7\frac{2}{7} \times \frac{7}{7}$ ☐ $7\frac{2}{7}$

13. $\frac{1}{3} \times 1\frac{2}{5}$ ☐ $1\frac{2}{5}$

14. $\frac{1}{3} \times 8\frac{2}{5}$ ☐ $8\frac{2}{5}$

15. $2\frac{3}{5} \times \frac{4}{4}$ ☐ $2\frac{3}{5}$

16. $9\frac{3}{5} \times \frac{3}{3}$ ☐ $9\frac{3}{5}$

17. $3\frac{1}{3} \times 4\frac{2}{7}$ ☐ $4\frac{2}{7}$

18. $1\frac{2}{3} \times 2\frac{2}{5}$ ☐ $2\frac{2}{5}$

19. $5\frac{1}{2} \times 6\frac{2}{3}$ ☐ $5\frac{1}{2}$

20. $3\frac{1}{3} \times \frac{4}{4}$ ☐ $3\frac{1}{3}$

21. Put the following products in order from least to greatest, without multiplying.

$5 \times \frac{3}{4}, \ 4\frac{1}{4} \times \frac{3}{4}, \ \frac{1}{2} \times \frac{3}{4}, \ \frac{3}{3} \times \frac{3}{4}$

_____

22. Put the following products in order from greatest to least, without multiplying.

$6 \times \frac{2}{5}, \ 3\frac{2}{3} \times \frac{2}{5}, \ \frac{2}{7} \times \frac{2}{5}, \ \frac{2}{2} \times \frac{2}{5}$

_____

23. Melissa and her friends are stretching rubber bands for an activity in science class. Melissa stretched her elastic to 10 inches. Juan stretched it $3\frac{1}{2}$ times as far. Sara stretched it $\frac{4}{4}$ as far. Marsha stretched it $\frac{2}{5}$ as far. Put the students in order of how far they stretched their rubber bands from least to greatest.

_____

Problem Solving: Multiple-Step Problems

Some word problems have hidden questions that must be answered before you can solve the problem.

A paved trail is 4 miles long. Jess runs $\frac{3}{8}$ of the length of the trail and walks the rest of the way. How many miles of the trail does Jess walk?

What do you know?	Jess runs $\frac{3}{8}$ of an 4-mile trail.
What are you asked to find?	How many miles of the trail that Jess walks.
How can you find the distance that Jess walks?	Subtract the distance Jess ran from the length of the trail.
What is the hidden question? The hidden question will help you find data you need to solve the problem.	How many miles did Jess run? To answer, find $\frac{3}{8} \times 4 = 1\frac{1}{2}$.

Use the data to solve: $4 - 1\frac{1}{2} = 2\frac{1}{2}$, so Jess walked $2\frac{1}{2}$ of the 4 miles.

Write and answer the hidden question(s) in each problem. Then solve the problem.

1. Jared surfed for $\frac{1}{3}$ of the 9 hours he was at the beach. He spent the rest of the time building a sand castle. How many hours did he spend building the castle?

   Hidden question:_____

   Solution:_____

2. April put gasoline in 4 of her 5-gallon cans and 6 of her 2-gallon cans. She filled all the cans to the exact capacity. How many gallons of gasoline did she buy?

   Hidden question 1:_____

   Hidden question 2:_____

   Solution:_____

3. It costs Le Stor $10 to buy a shirt. The store sells the shirt for $2\frac{1}{2}$ times its cost. What is the profit for 100 of these shirts? Hint: Profit equals sales minus cost.

   Hidden question 1:_____

   Hidden question 2:_____

   Solution:_____

Name _____

Problem Solving:
Multiple-Step Problems

Write and answer the hidden question(s) in each problem. Then solve the problem.

1. Rahm spent $2\frac{1}{2}$ hours writing an essay. It took him 4 times as long to finish his science project. How long did it take Rahm to write the essay and finish the science project?

   Hidden question(s):_____

   Solution:_____

2. Lauren bought 20 ounces of sliced ham. She used $\frac{3}{4}$ of the ham to make sandwiches for her friends and $\frac{1}{5}$ of the ham in an omelet. How many ounces of ham were left?

   Hidden question(s):_____

   Solution:_____

3. Sarah cut off $\frac{1}{8}$ of a 48-inch piece of ribbon. Jane cut off $\frac{1}{9}$ of a 36-inch piece of ribbon. They compared their cut pieces. Whose piece is longer? How much longer?

   Hidden question(s):_____

   Solution:_____

4. Misty bought 3 CDs. The country music CD cost $12. The rock music CD cost $\frac{2}{3}$ as much as the country music CD. The platinum edition CD cost twice as much as the rock CD. What was the cost of the three CDs?

   Hidden question(s):_____

   Solution:_____

5. Choose one of the problems above. Explain how you determined the hidden question and why it was necessary to answer that question in order to solve the problem.

   _____

   _____

   _____

Dividing Whole Numbers by Unit Fractions

How can you divide a whole number by a fraction?

$2 \div \frac{1}{3}$	Think: How can I divide two into one-thirds?
1. Two is the sum of one plus one. **2.** Each one is the sum of three one-thirds. **3.** Count the number of one-thirds. **Check** To divide a whole number by a fraction, multiply the whole number by the reciprocal of the fraction.	$2 \quad = \quad 1 \quad + \quad 1$ $\frac{1}{3} + \frac{1}{3} + \frac{1}{3} \quad + \quad \frac{1}{3} + \frac{1}{3} + \frac{1}{3}$ 6 $2 \div \frac{1}{3} = 2 \times \frac{3}{1} = \frac{2}{1} \times \frac{3}{1} = \frac{6}{1} = 6$

$3 \div \frac{3}{4}$	Think: How can I divide three into three-fourths?
1. Three is the sum of one plus one plus one. **2.** Each one is the sum of one three-fourths and one one-fourth. **3.** Count the number of three-fourths. **Check** Multiply the whole number by the reciprocal of the fraction.	$3 = \quad 1 \quad + \quad 1 \quad + \quad 1$ $\frac{3}{4} + \frac{1}{4} \quad + \quad \frac{3}{4} + \frac{1}{4} \quad + \quad \frac{3}{4} + \frac{1}{4}$ $\frac{3}{4} + \frac{3}{4} + \frac{3}{4} \quad + \quad \frac{1}{4} + \frac{1}{4} + \frac{1}{4}$ $\frac{3}{4} + \frac{3}{4} + \frac{3}{4} + \quad \frac{3}{4}$ 4 $3 \div \frac{3}{4} = 3 \times \frac{4}{3} = \frac{3}{1} \times \frac{4}{3} = \frac{12}{3} = 4$

Draw a picture that shows each division and write the answer.

1. $2 \div \frac{1}{2}$ _____

2. $2 \div \frac{1}{3}$ _____

Dividing Whole Numbers by Unit Fractions

In **1** and **2**, use the picture to find each quotient.

1. How many thirds are in 1?

_____

2. How many thirds are in 7?

_____

In **3** and **4**, draw a picture to find each quotient.

3. $3 \div \frac{1}{2}$

_____

4. $4 \div \frac{1}{8}$

_____

In **5** and **6**, use multiplication to find each quotient.

5. $6 \div \frac{1}{3}$

_____

6. $5 \div \frac{1}{10}$

_____

7. Julie bought 3 yards of cloth to make holiday napkin rings. If she needs $\frac{3}{4}$ of a yard to make each ring, how many rings can she make?

_____

8. When you divide a whole number by a fraction with a numerator of 1, explain how you can find the quotient.

_____

_____

_____

Name _____

Dividing Unit Fractions by Non-Zero Whole Numbers

How can you model dividing a unit fraction by a whole number?

Think: Divide $\frac{1}{3}$ into 4 equal parts.

$\frac{1}{3} \div 4$

Each part contains $\frac{1}{12}$ of the whole.

So $\frac{1}{3} \div 4 = \frac{1}{12}$.

Use multiplication to check.

$4 \times \frac{1}{12} = \frac{4}{12} = \frac{1}{3}$

Find the quotient.

1. $\frac{1}{2} \div 4$

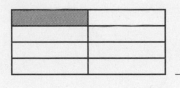

_____

2. $\frac{1}{4} \div 2$

_____

3. $\frac{1}{3} \div 6$ _____

4. $\frac{1}{5} \div 2$ _____

5. $\frac{1}{4} \div 5$ _____

6. $\frac{1}{6} \div 3$ _____

7. $\frac{1}{5} \div 7$ _____

8. $\frac{1}{2} \div 5$ _____

Name _____

Dividing Unit Fractions by Non-Zero Whole Numbers

In **1-16**, find the quotient.

1. $\frac{1}{4} \div 4$

2. $\frac{1}{3} \div 2$

(diagrams) ____ ____

3. $\frac{1}{2} \div 2$ _____   **4.** $\frac{1}{5} \div 4$ _____

5. $\frac{1}{4} \div 5$ _____   **6.** $\frac{1}{7} \div 7$ _____

7. $\frac{1}{6} \div 4$ _____   **8.** $\frac{1}{9} \div 6$ _____

9. $\frac{1}{2} \div 3$ _____   **10.** $\frac{1}{3} \div 5$ _____

11. $\frac{1}{4} \div 2$ _____   **12.** $\frac{1}{5} \div 7$ _____

13. $\frac{1}{6} \div 5$ _____   **14.** $\frac{1}{7} \div 6$ _____

15. $\frac{1}{2} \div 4$ _____   **16.** $\frac{1}{9} \div 5$ _____

17. Cameron and his family were eating leftover lasagna. There was $\frac{1}{2}$ of the lasagna left. Cameron has one brother, one sister, and two parents. If everyone gets the same size piece, what fraction of the original lasagna does each member of Cameron's family receive?

_____

_____

_____

Problem Solving: Draw a Picture and Write an Equation

Travis earned 3 stickers for each song he played in his piano lesson. He received a total of 24 stickers. How many songs did he play?

You can solve a problem like this by drawing a picture and writing an equation.

Step 1. Write out what you already know. Travis earned 3 stickers for each song he played. Travis had 24 stickers at the end of the lesson.

Step 2. Draw a picture to show what you know.

Travis's total stickers

Step 3. Write out what you are trying to find. How many songs did Travis play?

Step 4. Write an equation from your drawing. Since you are dividing Travis's total stickers into groups of 3 (stickers earned per song), this is a division problem.

$24 \div 3 = s$ s = number of songs Travis played

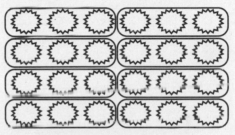

groups of 3 stickers Travis earned per song

Step 5. Solve the equation.

$24 \div 3 = 8$ $s = 8$
So, Travis played 8 songs during his lesson.

Step 6. Check your answer by working backward.

$8 \times 3 = 24$: your answer is correct.

Draw a picture, write an equation, and solve.

1. Sasha, Rudy, and Mario each have $1\frac{3}{4}$ cups of flour. Can they make a recipe for bread that needs 5 cups of flour?

_____

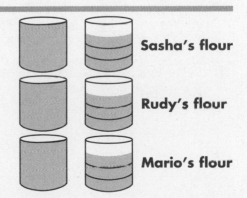

Sasha's flour

Rudy's flour

Mario's flour

Problem Solving: Draw a Picture and Write an Equation

Solve each problem. Draw a picture to show the main idea for each problem. Then write an equation and solve it. Write the answer in a complete sentence.

1. Bobby has 3 times as many model spaceships as his friend Sylvester does. Bobby has 21 spaceships. How many model spaceships does Sylvester have?

   _____

   _____

2. Dan saved $463 over the 12 weeks of summer break. He saved $297 of it during the last 4 weeks. How much did he save during the first 8 weeks?

   _____

   _____

3. Use a separate sheet of paper to show the main idea for the following problem. Choose the answer that solves the problem correctly.

   A box of peanut-butter crackers was divided evenly among 6 children. Each child got 9 crackers. How many crackers were in the box?

   A 54   **B** 48   **C** 39   **D** 36

4. Why is it helpful to draw a picture when attempting to solve an equation?

   _____

   _____

Solids

A **vertex** of a solid is the point at which three or more edges meet.

An **edge** of a solid is a line segment where two faces meet.

A **face** of a solid is a flat polygon-shaped surface.

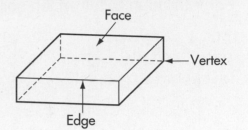

Face

Vertex

Edge

Here are some common three-dimensional shapes:

Cube   **Rectangular Prism**   **Cylinder**   **Cone**

For **1** through **3**, tell which solid each object resembles.

1. 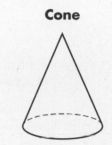 Art Supplies

_____

2. Soup

_____

3.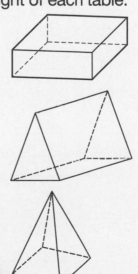

_____

In **4** through **6**, complete each table by writing the number of vertices, edges, and faces In each solid shown at the right of each table.

4.

Vertices	Edges	Faces

5.

Vertices	Edges	Faces

6.

Vertices	Edges	Faces

Name _____

Solids

For **1** through **3**, tell which solid each object resembles.

1. _____   2. _____   3. _____

For **4** and **5**, complete each table by writing the number of vertices, edges, and faces in each solid shown at the right of each table.

4.

Vertices	Edges	Faces

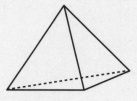

5.

Vertices	Edges	Faces

6. What is the name of the three-dimensional shape at the right?

   A Cone

   B Triangular prism

   C Pyramid

   D Rectangular prism

7. How many vertices does a cone have? Explain.

_____

_____

_____

_____

Name _____

Views of Solids

Here is what each figure on the left would look like from the front, side, and top. The number of cubes that can't be seen for each figure is written.

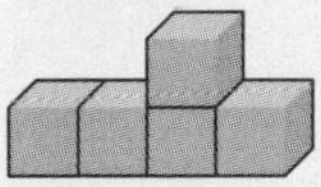

All the cubes are visible.

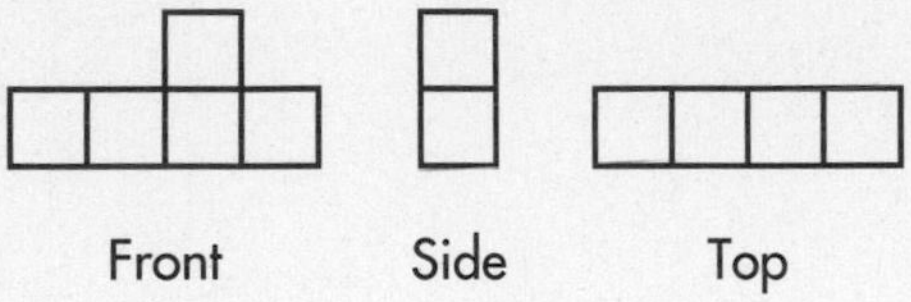

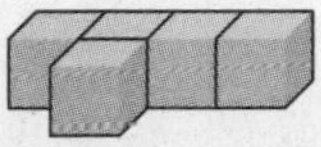

Front   Side   Top

All the cubes are visible.

Front   Side   Top

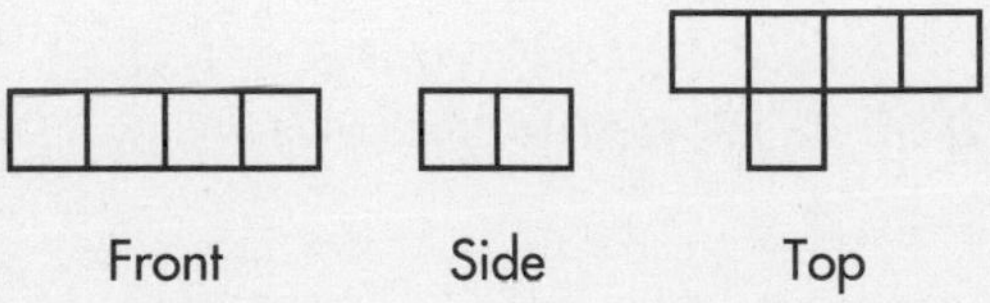

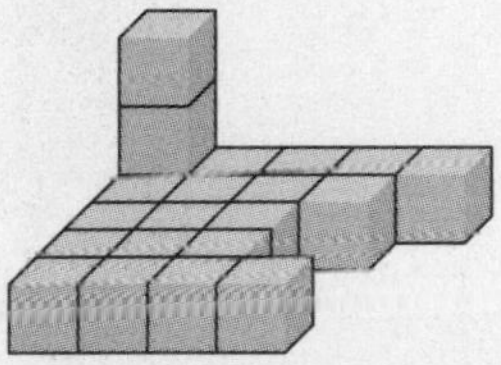

One of the cubes is not visible.

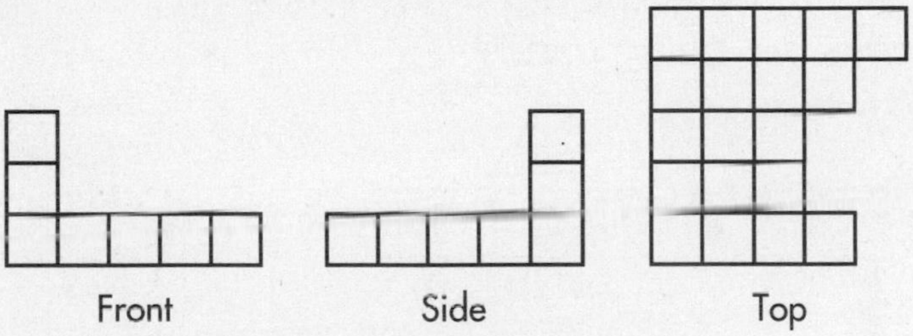

Front   Side   Top

Look at the figure. Label its front, side, and top views.

1.

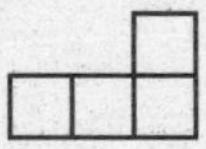

2.

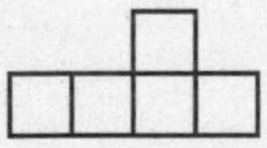

3.

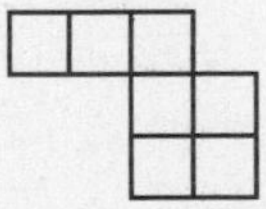

_____   _____   _____

How many cubes are hidden in each figure?

4.

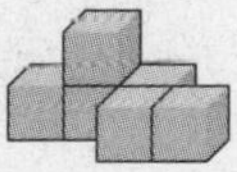

5.

6.

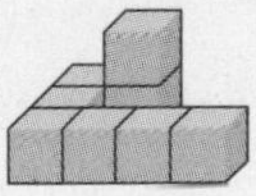

_____   _____   _____

Name _____

Views of Solids

For **1** and **2**, draw front, side, and top views of each stack of
unit blocks.

1.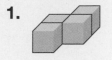

2.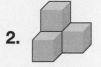

3. In the figure for Exercise **2**, how many blocks are not visible?

_____

4. In the figure at the right, how many unit
blocks are being used?

    A 8

    B 9

    C 10

    D 11

5. A figure is made from 8 unit blocks. It is 3 units tall. What is
the maximum length the figure could be? Explain.

_____

_____

_____

Name _____

Problem Solving: Use Objects and Solve a Simpler Problem

At a math fair, Willie saw a puzzle about a giant cube made of smaller identical white cubes. The giant cube was 4 × 4 × 4. It contained 64 smaller cubes. Each of the six faces of the giant cube was painted red. The puzzle asked, "If the giant cube were taken apart, how many smaller cubes would have only one face painted red?" Here is how Willie tried to solve the puzzle.

1. Construct Cube A using 8 smaller cubes and Cube B using 27 smaller cubes. Imagine painting Cubes A and B.

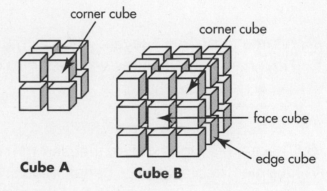

corner cube

corner cube

face cube

edge cube

Cube A   **Cube B**

2. Classify the smaller cubes. *Think: Where are the cubes located in the Cubes A and B? How are they painted differently from each other?* Make a table to organize the data.

Location	Cube A		Cube B	
	Number	**Painted Faces**	**Number**	**Painted Faces**
Corner	8	3	8	
Edge	none		12	
Face	none		6	
Center	none		1	

Willie organized the data about the 64 smaller cubes in the giant cube. Use the table above to complete the table below. One set of data has already been completed.

Giant Cube		
Painted Faces	**Location**	**Number**
3	Corner (*Think: Same as a 3 × 3 × 3.*)	8
2	Edge (*Think: One more than a 3 × 3 × 3 on each edge.*)	
1	Face (*Think: Three more than a 3 × 3 × 3 on each face.*)	
0	Center (*Think: The center is now 2 × 2 × 2.*)	

R 12·3

Problem Solving: Use Objects and Solve a Simpler Problem

Use objects to help you solve a simpler problem. Use the solution to help you solve the original problem.

1. Six people can be seated at a table. If two tables are put together, 10 people can be seated. How many tables are needed to make a long table that will seat 22 people?

_____

2. A large cube has 5 layers, each with 5 rows of 5 small cubes. How many small cubes will the larger cube contain?

_____

3. There are 5 kinds of fish that Jerome feeds: guppies, zebra danios, bettas, platys, and neon tetras. Use the following clues to find the order in which Jerome feeds them.

- Jerome feeds the guppies third.
- Jerome does not feed the bettas right before or right after the guppies.
- Jerome feeds the zebra danios last.
- Jerome feeds the platys after the bettas.

A Guppies, zebra danios, bettas, platys, and neon tetras

B Bettas, platys, guppies, neon tetras, zebra danios

C Neon tetras, zebra danios, guppies, platys, bettas

D Bettas, guppies, platys, neon tetras, zebra danios

4. Suppose Ann is placing bowling pins in the following manner: 1 pin in the first row, 2 pins in the second row, 3 pins in the third row, and so on. How many pins will she use if she has 5 rows in her placement? Explain.

_____

_____

Models and Volume

Volume is the measure of space inside a solid figure. If you had a box, the number of cubic units it would take to fill the box would be the volume.

Find the volume of this box in cubic units by counting the number of unit cubes.

There are 16 cubes in the front layer and there are two layers. The total number of unit cubes is 32.

So, the volume is 32 cubic units.

In **1** through **6**, find the volume in cubic units.

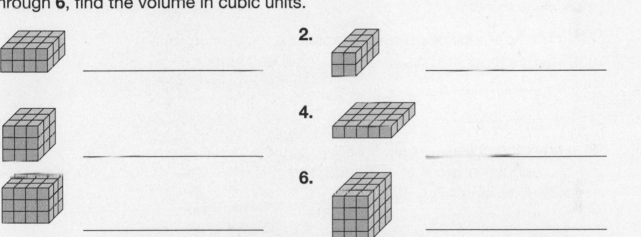

1. _____

2. _____

3. _____

4. _____

5. _____

6. _____

7. Draw a solid figure that has a volume of 10 cubic units.

8. A jewelry store received a package of rings that is 16 inches long, 10 inches wide, and 12 inches high. The package contains 1-inch cubes that each hold one ring. How many rings did the jewelry store receive? Explain how you found your answer.

_____

_____

_____

Models and Volume

Find the number of cubes needed to make each rectangular prism. You can use unit cubes or you can count the cubes by looking at the drawing.

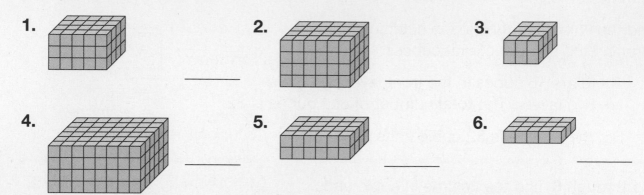

1. _____

2. _____

3. _____

4. _____

5. _____

6. _____

7. In the space below, draw a model of a rectangular prism 5 cubes long × 4 cubes wide × 2 cubes high.

8. How many cubes would it take to make a model of a rectangular prism that is 3 units long × 2 units wide × 4 units high?

   A 48   **B** 24   **C** 12   **D** 6

9. How can you find the volume of a rectangular prism using a model?

_____

_____

_____

_____

Volume

Volume is a measure of the space inside a solid figure. It is measured in cubic units. A **cubic unit** is the volume of a cube that has edges that are each 1 unit.

How to find the volume of a rectangular prism

Counting unit cubes:

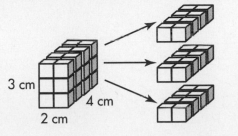

3 cm

4 cm

2 cm

Count the cubes in each layer: 8 cubes.

Multiply by the number of layers.

    8 cubes × 3 = 24 cubes

The volume of each cube is 1 cm³.

The volume of the prism is 24 cm³.

Using a formula:

You know the length ℓ, the width w, and the height h. Calculate the volume, V, using the formula $V = \ell \times w \times h$.

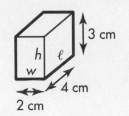

h ℓ

w

3 cm

4 cm

2 cm

$V = 4 \text{ cm} \times 2 \text{ cm} \times 3 \text{ cm}$

$V = 24 \text{ cm}^3$

Find the volume of each rectangular prism using a formula.

1.

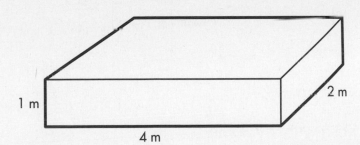

1 m

2 m

4 m

2.

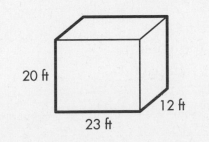

20 ft

12 ft

23 ft

Volume

Find the volume of each rectangular prism.

1. base area 56 in^2, height 6 in.   _____

2. base area 32 cm^2, height 12 cm   _____

3. base area 42 m^2, height 8 m   _____

4.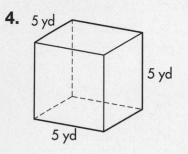

5.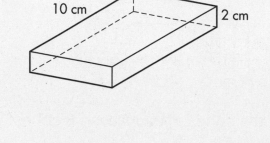

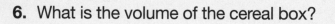

6. What is the volume of the cereal box?

_____

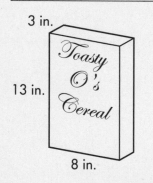

7. What is the volume of this solid?

A 3.2 m^3 **C** 320 m^3

B 32 m^3 **D** 3,200 m^3

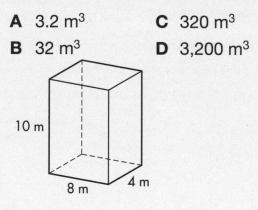

8. What is the height of a solid with a volume
   of 120 m^3 and base area of 30 m^2?   _____

9. Bradford has an aquarium with a base that is
   22 inches × 12 inches and a height that is 15 inches.
   What is the volume of the aquarium? Would the volume
   of the aquarium change if it did not have a lid? Explain.

_____

_____

_____

Combining Volumes

To find the volume of a solid made up of familiar parts, find the
volume of each part and add the volumes.

Step 1: To find the volume of the figure at the
right, separate the solid into two rectangular
prisms. (See the dotted line in the figure.)

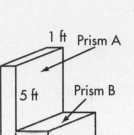

Step 2: Use the formula
$V = \ell \times w \times h$ to find
the volume of each prism.

Volume of Prism A

$V = 1 \times 4 \times 7 = 28 \text{ ft}^3$

Volume of Prism B

$V = 2 \times 4 \times 2 = 16 \text{ ft}^3$

Step 3: Add the volumes
of each prism.

The volume of the solid is $28 + 16 = 44 \text{ ft}^3$.

---

1. Show two ways of dividing the given solid into two rectangular solids.

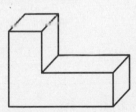

2. Find the volume of the rectangular solid shown below. Show your work.

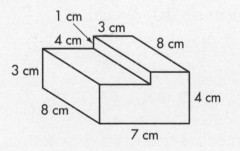

_____

_____

Name _____

Combining Volumes

For **1** through **4**, find the volume of each solid figure.

1.

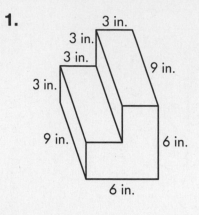

3 in.
3 in.
3 in.
9 in.
3 in.
9 in.
6 in.
6 in.

2.

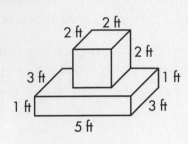

2 ft
2 ft
2 ft
3 ft
1 ft
1 ft
3 ft
5 ft

_____

3.

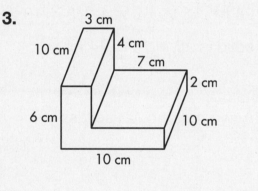

3 cm
4 cm
10 cm
7 cm
2 cm
6 cm
10 cm
10 cm

4.

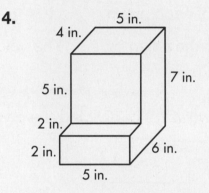

5 in.
4 in.
7 in.
5 in.
2 in.
2 in.
6 in.
5 in.

_____

5. Paul wants to build this model with clay, but he does not know how many cubic centimeters of clay to purchase. How much clay should he purchase?

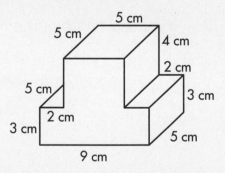

5 cm
5 cm
4 cm
2 cm
5 cm
3 cm
2 cm
3 cm
5 cm
9 cm

   A 235 cm³   **C** 405 cm³

   B 335 cm³   **D** 935 cm³

6. Ashley is stacking two boxes on a shelf. The bottom box measures 6 inches × 5 inches × 5 inches. The top box is a cube with one edge measuring 4 inches. What is the volume of this stack? Explain how you found your answer.

_____

_____

Name _____

Problem Solving:
Use Objects and Reasoning

This cube has a volume of 1 cm³.

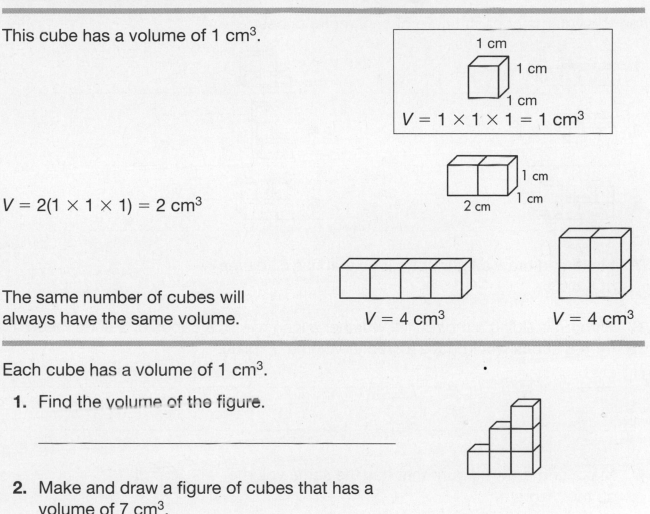

1 cm
1 cm
1 cm
$V = 1 \times 1 \times 1 = 1 \text{ cm}^3$

$V = 2(1 \times 1 \times 1) = 2 \text{ cm}^3$

1 cm
1 cm
2 cm

The same number of cubes will always have the same volume.

$V = 4 \text{ cm}^3$

$V = 4 \text{ cm}^3$

Each cube has a volume of 1 cm³.

1. Find the volume of the figure.

_____

2. Make and draw a figure of cubes that has a volume of 7 cm³.

3. Explain how you knew how many cubes to use to draw the figure in Exercise 2.

_____

4. Find the volume.

_____

5. If the cubes in Exercise 4 were increased to 3 cm on a side, how would the volume be affected?

_____

_____

Name _____

Problem Solving:
Use Objects and Reasoning

Find the volume of each figure of centimeter cubes.

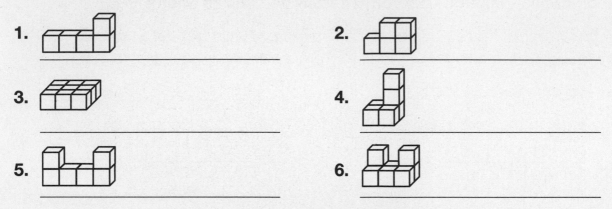

1. _____

2. _____

3. _____

4. _____

5. _____

6. _____

7. Make and draw a figure of cubes that has a volume of 6 cm³.

8. Without building a model, tell whether a long row of 8 cubes or a cube made from 8 cubes would have a greater volume. Explain.

_____

_____

9. Make and draw a figure that has the same volume as the diagram.

10. Find the volume of these figures. Then describe the pattern(s) you see. Can you determine the volume of the next figure in the pattern? Explain.

_____

_____

_____

_____

Converting Customary Units of Length

How to change a length measurement from one unit to another:

Converting a length measurement from a smaller unit to a larger unit

6 feet = _____ yards

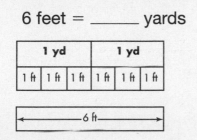

Think: If I measure the same length using a larger unit, I will need a smaller number of units.

Operation: Divide.

You know 3 ft = 1 yd.

Find $6 \div 3$; 6 ft = 2 yd

Converting a length measurement from a larger unit to a smaller unit

2 feet = _____ inches

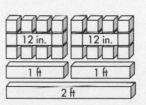

Think: If I measure the same length using a smaller unit, I will need a larger number of units.

Operation: Multiply.

You know 1 ft = 12 in.

Find 2×12; 2 ft = 24 in.

Relationships Among Customary Units of Length			
Inch	Foot	Yard	Mile
12 in. =	1 ft		
36 in. =	3 ft =	1 yd	
	5,280 ft =	1,760 yd =	1 mi

Complete.

1. 5 ft = _____ in.

2. 3 mi = _____ ft

3. 108 in. = _____ ft

4. 72 in. = _____ yd

5. 2 ft 3 in. = _____ in.

6. 45 in. = _____ yd _____ in.

7. Which is the greater length, 2 yards or 5 feet? _____

8. **Estimation** A creek runs along a distance of 16,300 feet. About how many miles long is the creek? _____

Name _____

Converting Customary Units of Length

Convert each unit.

1. 12 yd = _____ in.

2. 30 ft = _____ yd

3. 75 ft = _____ in.

4. 10 ft 7 in. = _____ in.

5. 6 mi = _____ ft

6. 2 mi = _____ yd

Write >, =, or < for each ◯.

7. 64 in. ◯ 5 ft

8. 2 mi ◯ 3,333 yd

9. 36 yd 2 ft ◯ 114 ft 2 in.

The Statue of Liberty was a gift to the United States from the people of France. Some of the dimensions of the statue are shown here.

Measurements of the Statue of Liberty	
Height from base of statue to the torch	151 ft 1 in.
Length of hand	16 ft 5 in.
Length of index finger	8 ft
Length of nose	4 ft 6 in.
Thickness of right arm	12 ft

10. What is the height, from the base of the statue to the torch, in inches? _____

11. What is the thickness of the statue's right arm in yards? _____

12. Which measure is less than 435 inches?

   A 37 ft   **B** 36 ft 10 in.   **C** 12 yd 3 in.   **D** 12 ft 3 in.

13. Explain how you can find the number of feet in 40 yards.

_____

_____

Converting Customary Units of Capacity

How to change a capacity measurement from one unit to another

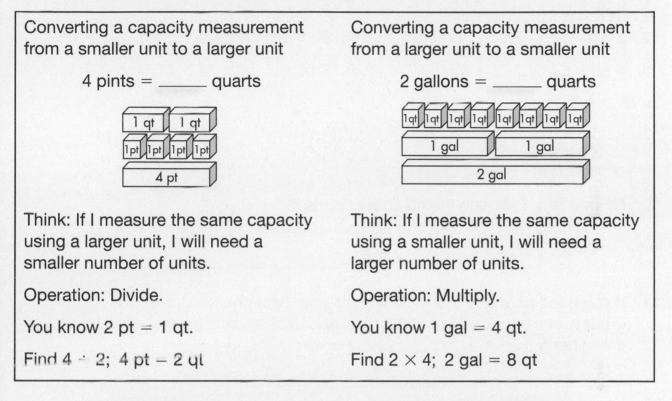

Converting a capacity measurement from a smaller unit to a larger unit

4 pints = _____ quarts

Think: If I measure the same capacity using a larger unit, I will need a smaller number of units.

Operation: Divide.

You know 2 pt = 1 qt.

Find 4 ÷ 2; 4 pt = 2 qt

Converting a capacity measurement from a larger unit to a smaller unit

2 gallons = _____ quarts

Think: If I measure the same capacity using a smaller unit, I will need a larger number of units.

Operation: Multiply.

You know 1 gal = 4 qt.

Find 2 × 4; 2 gal = 8 qt

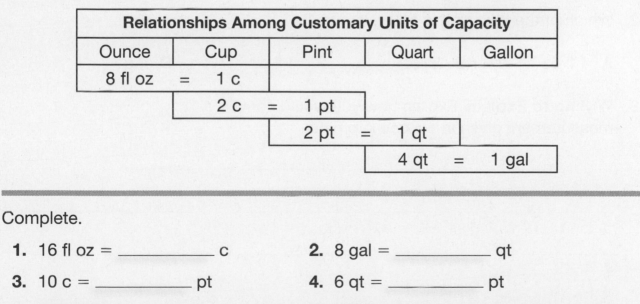

Relationships Among Customary Units of Capacity				
Ounce	Cup	Pint	Quart	Gallon
8 fl oz =	1 c			
	2 c =	1 pt		
		2 pt =	1 qt	
			4 qt =	1 gal

Complete.

1. 16 fl oz = _____ c

2. 8 gal = _____ qt

3. 10 c = _____ pt

4. 6 qt = _____ pt

5. Estimation A vat has a capacity of 642 fl oz. Estimate its capacity in cups.

_____

Name _____

Converting Customary Units of Capacity

Convert each unit.

1. 2 qt = _____ pt

2. 5 c = _____ pt _____ c

3. 3 gal = _____ pt

4. 96 fl oz = _____ c

5. 4 qt = _____ c

6. 9 pt = _____ c

Solve.

7.   5 c 4 fl oz
        − 4 c 3 fl oz
        _____

8.   7 gal 2 qt
        + 3 gal 1 qt
        _____

9.   6 qt 1 pt
        − 2 qt 1 pt
        _____

10. Estimation Estimate the number of pints in 445 ounces.

_____

11. If you needed only 1 c of milk, what is your best choice at the grocery store—a quart container, a pint container, or a $\frac{1}{2}$ gal container?

_____

12. Which of the following is equivalent to 1 c?

A 4 fl oz   **B** 2 pt   **C** 8 fl oz   **D** 4 qt

13. Writing to Explain Explain how you would convert a measurement given in ounces into pints.

_____

_____

_____

Name _____

Reteaching
13-3

Converting Customary Units of Weight

How to change a weight measurement from one unit to another:

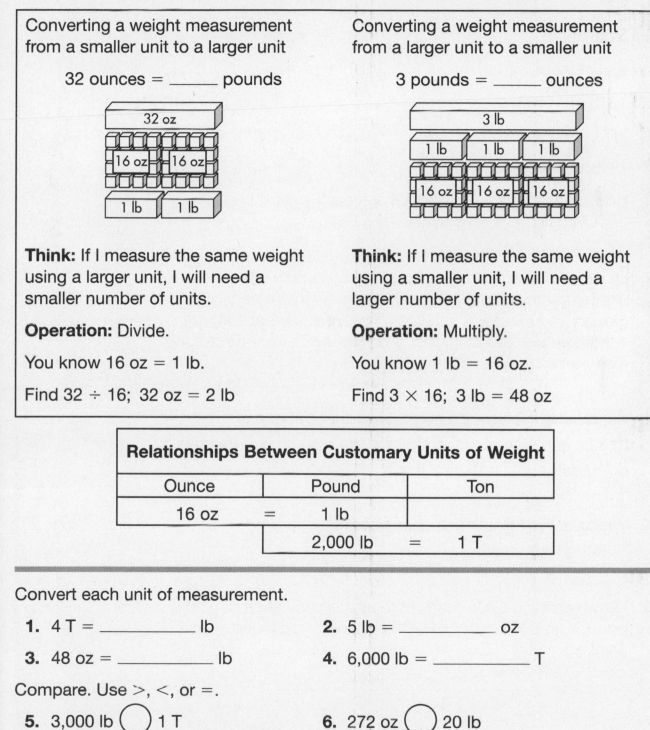

Converting a weight measurement from a smaller unit to a larger unit

32 ounces = _____ pounds

Think: If I measure the same weight using a larger unit, I will need a smaller number of units.

Operation: Divide.

You know 16 oz = 1 lb.

Find 32 ÷ 16; 32 oz = 2 lb

Converting a weight measurement from a larger unit to a smaller unit

3 pounds = _____ ounces

Think: If I measure the same weight using a smaller unit, I will need a larger number of units.

Operation: Multiply.

You know 1 lb = 16 oz.

Find 3 × 16; 3 lb = 48 oz

Relationships Between Customary Units of Weight		
Ounce	Pound	Ton
16 oz =	1 lb	
	2,000 lb =	1 T

Convert each unit of measurement.

1. 4 T = _____ lb

2. 5 lb = _____ oz

3. 48 oz = _____ lb

4. 6,000 lb = _____ T

Compare. Use >, <, or =.

5. 3,000 lb ◯ 1 T

6. 272 oz ◯ 20 lb

7. Estimation A candy maker buys a bar of chocolate weighing 162 ounces. About how many pounds does the bar weigh?

_____

Name _____

Converting Customary Units of Weight

Convert each unit of measurement.

1. 8 T = _____ lb

2. $2\frac{1}{2}$ lb = _____ oz

3. 4,000 lb = _____ T

4. 90 lb = _____ oz

Compare. Use >, <, or =.

5. 16 lb ◯ 16 oz

6. 1,500 lb ◯ 2 T

7. 3 T ◯ 5,999 lb

8. 1,600 oz ◯ 10 lb

9. 19 lb ◯ 300 oz

10. 8 oz ◯ $\frac{1}{2}$ lb

11. How many ounces of potatoes are in a 5-pound bag of potatoes?

_____

12. Did you know that there is litter in outer space? Humans exploring space have left behind bags of trash, bolts, gloves, and pieces of satellites. There are currently about 4,000,000 pounds of litter in orbit around Earth. About how many tons of space litter is this?

_____

13. Karla bought 2 pounds of red beads, $1\frac{3}{4}$ pounds of green beads, and 10 ounces of string at the craft store. How much do Karla's supplies weigh in all?

_____

14. Which of the following is equivalent to $92\frac{1}{2}$ pounds?

   A 1,472 oz   B 1,480 oz   C 1,479 oz   D 1,488 oz

15. How much is $3\frac{1}{2}$ pounds written as a combination of whole pounds and whole ounces? Explain how you found your answer.

_____

_____

_____

Converting Metric Units of Length

How to change a length measurement from one metric unit to another:

Converting a length from a smaller to a larger metric unit

200 centimeters = _____ meters

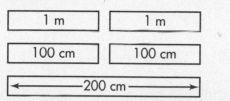

Think: If I measure the same length using a larger unit, I will need a smaller number of units.

Operation: Divide.

You know 100 cm = 1 m.

Find 200 ÷ 100; 200 cm = 2 m

Converting a length from a larger to a smaller metric unit

2 kilometers = _____ meters

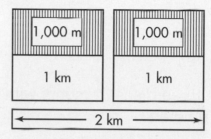

Think: If I measure the same length using a smaller unit, I will need a larger number of units.

Operation: Multiply.

You know 1 km = 1,000 m.

Find 2 × 1,000; 2 km = 2,000 m

Relationships Among Metric Units of Length						
Kilometer			Meter		Centimeter	Millimeter
1 km	=		1,000 m			
			1 m	=	100 cm =	1,000 mm
					1 cm =	10 mm

Complete.

1. 80 mm = _____ cm

2. 234 cm = _____ mm

3. 2 m = _____ mm

4. 14,000 mm = _____ m

5. Which is shorter, 60 meters or 600 centimeters? _____

6. Is 3.2 meters equal to 320 millimeters? Explain.

Converting Metric Units of Length

Convert each unit.

1. 25 m = _____ cm

2. 345 cm = _____ m

3. 4.5 m = _____ cm

4. 10 m = _____ mm

5. 987 mm = _____ cm

6. 4,000 mm = _____ cm

7. 4.2 km = _____ m

8. 3 km = _____ m

9. List three measurements with different units that are equal to 5 meters.

_____

Write >, =, or < for each ◯.

10. 12 cm ◯ 98 mm

11. 3 km ◯ 5,000 m

12. 800 cm ◯ 8 m

13. 38.5 mm ◯ 10 cm

14. 9,000 cm ◯ 2 km

15. 1,000,000 mm ◯ 100 m

Mount Saint Helens, a volcano, erupted on May 18, 1980.
Before the eruption, Mount St. Helens was 2,950 meters high.
After the eruption, it was 2,550 meters high.

16. What is the difference in height of Mount St. Helens before and after the eruption, expressed in meters? _____

17. Before the eruption, how many kilometers high was Mount St. Helens? _____

18. Which of the following is equal to 2 meters?

A 200 mm   **B** 20 cm   **C** 200 km   **D** 2,000 mm

19. Explain how you would convert 4 m to millimeters.

_____

_____

Converting Metric Units of Capacity

How to change a capacity measurement from one metric unit to another:

Converting a capacity from a smaller to a larger metric unit

2,000 milliliters = _____ liters

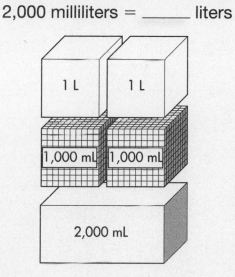

Think: If I measure the same capacity using a larger unit, I will need a smaller number of units.

Operation: Divide.

You know 1,000 mL = 1 L.

Find 2,000 ÷ 1,000; 2,000 mL = 2 L

Converting a capacity from a larger to a smaller metric unit

3 liters = _____ milliliters

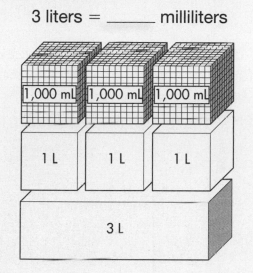

Think: If I measure the same capacity using a smaller unit, I will need a larger number of units.

Operation: Multiply.

You know 1 L = 1,000 mL.

Find 3 × 1,000; 3 L = 3,000 mL

Relationships Between Metric Units of Capacity			
Liter			Millimeter
1 L	=		1,000 mL

Complete.

1. 6 L = _____ mL

2. 4,000 mL = _____ L

3. 8,000 mL = _____ L

4. 91,000 mL = _____ L

Estimation Circle the capacity that is most reasonable for each container.

5. soup bowl

2 L   or   300 mL

6. bathtub

200 L   or   34,000 mL

Converting Metric Units of Capacity

Convert each unit.

1. 5 L = _____ mL

2. 13,000 mL = _____ L

3. 16 L = _____ mL

4. 4,000 mL = _____ L

5. 9,000 mL = _____ L

6. 8 L = _____ mL

7. You are preparing for a breakfast party and need enough milk for 20 people. Each person will drink about 200 mL of milk. Which is the best estimate of the amount of milk you should prepare: 400 mL or 4 L? Why?

_____

Which capacity is most reasonable for each container?

8. coffee mug   300 mL or 3 L   _____

9. vase   20 mL or 2 L   _____

10. cleaning bucket   500 mL or 5 L   _____

11. Which of the following is equal to 6,000 mL?

A 6 L   **B** 60 L   **C** 600 L   **D** 60,000 L

12. Writing to Explain Suppose you have a 100-mL cup, a 300-mL cup, and a 500-mL cup. List two different ways you can measure exactly 1 L.

_____

_____

_____

Converting Metric Units of Mass

How to convert a mass measurement from one metric unit to another:

Converting a mass from a smaller to a larger metric unit

6,000 grams = _____ kilograms

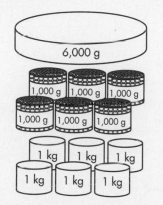

Think: If I measure the same mass using a larger unit, I will need a smaller number of units.

Operation: Divide.

You know 1,000 g = 1 kg.

Find 6,000 ÷ 1,000; 6,000 g = 6 kg

Converting a mass from a larger to a smaller metric unit

2 grams = _____ milligrams

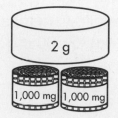

Think: If I measure the same mass using a smaller unit, I will need a larger number of units.

Operation: Multiply.

You know 1 g = 1,000 mg.

Find 2 × 1,000; 2 g = 2,000 mg

Relationships Between Metric Units of Mass					
Kilogram			Gram		Milligram
1 kg	=		1,000 g		
			1g	=	1,000 mg

Convert each unit of measurement.

1. 72 g = _____ mg

2. 8,000 g = _____ kg

3. 2,000,000 mg = _____ kg

4. 2,340 kg = _____ g

Compare. Use <, >, or =.

5. 4,000 mg ◯ 5 g

6. 64 kg ◯ 64,000 g

7. 3 kg ◯ 40,000 mg

8. 5,000 g ◯ 4 kg

Converting Metric Units of Mass

Convert each unit of measurement.

1. 15,000 g = _____ kg

2. 285 kg = _____ g

3. 5,000 mg = _____ g

4. 7,000 g = _____ kg

5. 490,000 g = _____ kg

6. 648 g = _____ mg

7. Order the following masses from least to greatest:
500 g, 50 kg, 5,000 mg

_____

Compare. Use $<$, $>$, or $=$.

8. 55,000 mg $\bigcirc$ 5 kg

9. 20 g $\bigcirc$ 2 kg

10. 11 g $\bigcirc$ 1,100 mg

11. 4,000 mg $\bigcirc$ 4 g

12. What is the value of x?　　40,000 mg = 10x g

A 400　　　　　**B** 40　　　　　**C** 4　　　　　**D** 0.4

13. A recipe that serves two people calls for 1,600 milligrams of baking soda. You want to make enough for 10 people. How much baking soda will you need, in grams?

_____

14. You want to convert 1 kilogram to milligrams. You already know that 1 kilogram = 1,000 grams. Explain how knowing that 1 gram = 1,000 milligrams can help you.

_____

_____

_____

Name _____

Problem Solving:
Multiple-Step Problems

Kyle hiked 10 miles on Saturday. He hiked half as many miles on Sunday. How many total yards did Kyle hike?

1. What am I asked to find?

2. What is the hidden question?

3. What is the answer to the hidden question?

4. What else do you need to do?

1. Total yards hiked

2. Number of miles hiked on Sunday

3. 5 miles

4. Convert from miles to yards

Solve.

Think: to convert from larger units to smaller units, use multiplication.

You know 1 mi = 1,760 yd. How many yd is 10 mi? _____

How many yd is 5 mi? _____

How many yd is 15 mi? _____

So, Kyle hiked a total of _____ _____

1. Mental Math Kendra biked 10 kilometers on Monday. She biked twice that many km on Tuesday. How many total meters did she bike? What hidden question do you need to answer? Show your work.

_____

_____

_____

Problem Solving:
Multiple-Step Problems

Answer the hidden question or questions. Then solve.

1. Isabel took 24 minutes to run around the track 6 times.
   John took 3 minutes to run around the track once. Which
   student was running faster?

   _____

   _____

   _____

2. Nancy is saving $2 from her allowance every week. Marco
   is saving $1 the first week, $2 the second week, $3 the third
   week, and so on. At the end of 10 weeks, who will have
   saved more money? How much more?

   _____

   _____

3. For every 3 cans of vegetables purchased, you get 1 free
   can. Tessie went home with 32 cans of vegetables. How
   many did she have to pay for?

   A 32   **B** 24   **C** 16   **D** 8

4. **Writing to Explain** Badal has 120 cm³ of water. He wants to
   pour it into a rectangular vase that is 4 cm high, 4 cm wide,
   and 5 cm long. Can he pour all the water into the vase? Explain.

   _____

   _____

   _____

Line Plots

The table below gives the number of miles Freda ran over a period of days. A line plot shows data along a number line. Each *X* represents one number in the data set.

Miles Run	Days
2	2
3	4
4	5
5	3
6	2
12	1

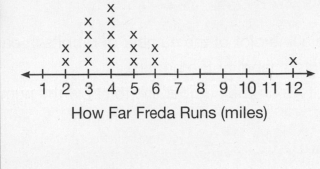

How Far Freda Runs (miles)

On the line plot, each *X* represents 1 day. An outlier is a number in a data set that is very different from the rest of the numbers.

1. Is there an outlier in the data set above? Explain.

_____

2. Complete the line plot to show the data in the table for puppies' weights at birth. Identify the outlier in the data set.

_____

Weight (lb)	Number of Puppies
3	5
4	3
5	2
6	0
7	1
13	1

```
←+—+—+—+—+—+—+—+—+—+—+→
  3  4  5  6  7  8  9 10 11 12 13
     Weights of Puppies (lb)
```

Line Plots

Number of Rabbits in Each Litter	1	2	3	4	5	6	7	8	9	10	11	12
Litters	/	///	////	//// ////	//// //	//// ///	////	////	///	////	///	/

1. Make a line plot of the number of rabbits in each litter.

   a. Write a label at the bottom.

   b. Put *X*s on the number line to show the number of rabbits in a litter.

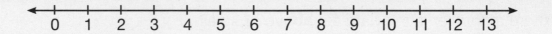

2. How many *X*s are shown for 6? _____

3. What is the number of rabbits that appears in a litter most often?

   A 3 rabbits   **B** 4 rabbits   **C** 5 rabbits   **D** 6 rabbits

4. Is the 1-rabbit litter an outlier?

   _____

   _____

Data from Surveys

In a survey, each student was asked this question. What color is your math notebook? Here are the responses: red, blue, green, red, yellow, yellow, red, blue, red, yellow, blue.

How to display data collected from surveys:

The data can be displayed in a frequency table or a line plot.

Frequency Table	**Line Plot**
1. Count the number of times each different response was made. red: ////; blue: ///; green: /; yellow: ///	1. Count the number of times each different response was made. red: ////; blue: ///; green: /; yellow: ///
2. Construct a frequency table. The table lists each response and its frequency. (The frequency of a response is how many times it was made.)	2. Construct a line plot. The plot lists each response along a horizontal line. The frequencies are stacked as x's above each response.
3. Give the frequency table a title that clearly explains what information is in the table.	3. Give the line plot a title that clearly explains what information is in the plot.

Survey Question:
What color is your math notebook?

Notebook Color	Number
Red	4
Blue	3
Green	1
Yellow	3

Survey Question:
What color Is your math notebook?

```
 x
 x         x                   x
 x         x                   x
 x         x         x         x
 +---------+---------+---------+
Red      Blue     Green    Yellow
```

1. How many students responded to the notebook survey? _____

2. Which color are the greatest number of math notebooks? _____

3. Describe how you might pick a sample of 50 minivan owners that represent the minivan owners of your state.

_____

_____

Data from Surveys

Ms. Chen's class took a survey on how many minutes it took each student to get to school. The results are below:

12   14   5   22   18   12   12   6   14   18   12   5   11

1. What are the highest and lowest times?   _____

2. Make a line plot
to display the data.

Students in Ms. Chen's Class

Music Bought in Class B

```
                                      x
                                      x         x
          x           x               x         x
          x           x               x         x
          x           x       x       x         x
        ────────────────────────────────────────────
         Rock       R & B  Classical Alternative Country
```
CDs Bought

3. If the entire class responded to the survey,
how many students are in the class?   _____

4. What information was collected about music? _____

_____

5. Use the line plot above. Which type of CDs did students
buy most often?

A Alternative   **B** Classical   **C** Country   **D** Rock

6. Write a survey question that might gather the following information. "In
one school there are 6 sets of twins, 2 sets of triplets, and one set of
quadruplets."

_____

_____

Making Line Plots

Joshua surveyed his classmates to collect data on their shoe sizes. He found the following information.

$7\frac{1}{2}$	7	$5\frac{1}{2}$	$6\frac{1}{2}$
$8\frac{1}{2}$	6	$7\frac{1}{2}$	$5\frac{1}{2}$
6	$7\frac{1}{2}$	$5\frac{1}{2}$	6
$6\frac{1}{2}$	6	8	6
$7\frac{1}{2}$	$7\frac{1}{2}$	8	$7\frac{1}{2}$

When you want to organize the data into a line plot, first organize the data. List the shoe sizes from least to greatest. Fill in the missing data below.

$5\frac{1}{2}$, 6, _____, 7, _____, _____, _____

Then make a table to show the frequency of the values.

Shoe Size	Tally	Frequency
$5\frac{1}{2}$		
6		
7		

Now draw a line plot.

Shoe Sizes

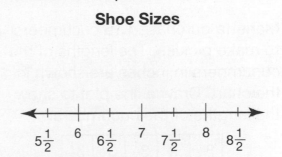

For questions **1–2**, draw a line plot.

1.

$13\frac{1}{2}$	13	$14\frac{1}{4}$	$13\frac{1}{2}$	13
$14\frac{1}{4}$	$14\frac{1}{2}$	$14\frac{1}{2}$	13	$14\frac{1}{2}$

2.

$2\frac{1}{2}$	5	$2\frac{3}{4}$	$4\frac{1}{4}$	5
$2\frac{3}{4}$	$4\frac{1}{2}$	$4\frac{1}{2}$	5	$4\frac{1}{2}$
$4\frac{1}{4}$	5	5	$4\frac{1}{4}$	$4\frac{1}{4}$
$4\frac{1}{4}$	$4\frac{1}{2}$	$4\frac{1}{2}$		

Making Line Plots

1. Which statement best describes the heights of the giraffes shown in the line plot?

Giraffe Heights (in feet)

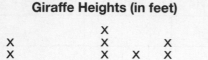

```
                    x
    x               x           x
    x               x   x       x
  ←─┼───────┼───────┼───────┼──→
   15      16      17      18
```

A The shortest giraffe is $16\frac{1}{4}$ feet tall.

B The tallest giraffe is $17\frac{1}{2}$ feet tall.

C Most of the giraffes are 17 feet tall.

D There are four giraffes in the data set.

3. Draw a line plot to represent the data in the table.

Value	Tally	Frequency
$5\frac{1}{4}$	|||	3
$6\frac{3}{4}$	||	2
$7\frac{1}{8}$	|||||	5
$7\frac{1}{2}$	||	2
$8\frac{1}{4}$	||	2

2. Marietta purchased 15 cucumbers to make pickles. The lengths of the cucumbers in inches are shown in the chart. Draw a line plot to show the lengths of the cucumbers.

$3\frac{1}{2}$	3	$3\frac{1}{4}$	$3\frac{1}{4}$	$3\frac{1}{2}$
$3\frac{3}{4}$	$3\frac{1}{2}$	$3\frac{1}{4}$	$3\frac{1}{2}$	$3\frac{3}{4}$
$3\frac{1}{4}$	$3\frac{1}{2}$	3	$3\frac{1}{4}$	$3\frac{1}{4}$

4. Write a frequency chart that matches the data in the line plot.

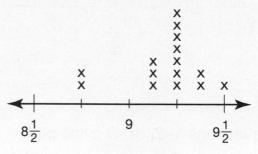

```
                        x
                        x
                        x
                        x
                x       x
        x       x   x   x
        x       x   x   x   x
    ←───┼───────┼───────┼───→
       8 1/2    9      9 1/2
```

5. Writing to Explain Write a description of the data in the line plot.

_____

_____

Name _____

Measurement Data

You have learned how to draw line plots. Now you can analyze
the data in a line plot. Mrs. Calderwood separated the rock samples
in her science classroom using their densities. She made a line
plot of the data.

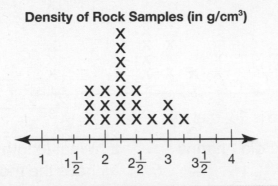

Density of Rock Samples (in g/cm³)

For questions **1–4**, use the line plot above.

1. Find how many rocks were used in the line plot.

_____

2. Which density occurs most often?

_____

3. What is the difference between the greatest density and
the least density?

_____

4. Monique says that $3\frac{1}{4}$ g/cm³ is an outlier. Is she right or
wrong? Explain.

_____

_____

_____

Measurement Data

Arianna counted the different sized bandages in her first aid kit.
She made a line plot of the data. Use this line plot to answer
the questions.

Lengths of Bandages (inches)

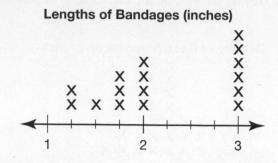

1. How many bandages did Arianna
   count?

   _____

2. What length bandage does Arianna
   have the most of?

   _____

3. Write an equation to show the total length of the bandages if they are placed
   end-to-end.

   _____

   _____

Madison sorted the earrings in her jewelry box.
The line plot shows the lengths of each post.

Lengths of Earring Posts (inches)

4. Write a statement to describe Madison's jewelry.

   _____

   _____

5. Why do you think that there are an even number
   of earring posts?

   _____

   _____

6. Make an educated guess as to why most of the posts are $\frac{3}{8}$-inch long.

   _____

   _____

Name _____

Problem Solving: Writing to Explain

Every Wednesday after Della comes home from school she attends a violin lesson, gets a ride to and from the lesson, and has a snack before going to the lesson. The line graph below gives more specific data about how Della spends her time and how far she travels from home after school on a Wednesday.

Looking at where the points are plotted on the graph can help you decide how Della spent her time. This data can help you write a story about how Della spent her Wednesday afternoon.

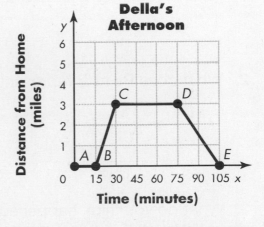

Story:
Della comes home and sits down to have a snack for 15 minutes. After this she gets a ride to her violin lesson which is 3 miles away. Della spends 45 minutes at the lesson. She gets another ride home that lasts for 30 minutes.

For **1** through **3**, use the High School Car Wash graph. Students at Larkin High School had a car wash to raise funds for the music club. The car wash began at 11:00 A.M.

1. Look at Point *A*. How many cars were washed in the first 20 minutes?

   _____

2. Look at Point *B*. How many more cars were washed in the next 20 minutes?

   _____

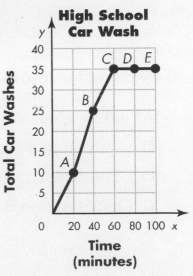

3. Write a story to fit the data on the graph.

   _____

   _____

   _____

Name _____

Problem Solving: Writing to Explain

For **1** through **5**, use the graph below.
The graph shows Cindy's errands.

1. Look at the coordinates at Point *A*.
   What does Point *A* represent?

   _____

   _____

2. What does Point *B* represent?

   _____

   _____

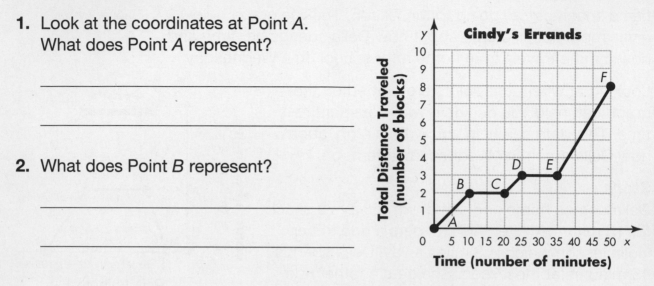

Cindy's Errands

3. What do you think happened between Points *B* and *C*?

   _____

   _____

   _____

4. Which of the following statements is supported by the graph?

   A Ten minutes occurred between Points *B* and *C*.

   B Cindy stopped for different amounts of time.

   C Cindy spent more time stopping than walking.

   D Cindy traveled 8 blocks in 30 minutes.

5. Write a complete story to match the data from the graph.

   _____

   _____

   _____

P 14·5

Polygons

A polygon is a closed plane figure made up of line segments. Common polygons have names that tell the number of sides the polygon has.

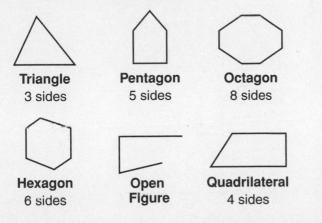

Triangle
3 sides

Pentagon
5 sides

Octagon
8 sides

Hexagon
6 sides

Open Figure

Quadrilateral
4 sides

A **regular polygon** has sides of equal length and angles of equal measure.

60°
3 in.   3 in.
60°   60°
3 in.

Each side is 3 in. long.
Each angle is 60°.

Name each polygon. Then tell if it appears to be a regular polygon.

1. _____
_____

2. _____
_____

3. _____
_____

4. _____
_____

5. Shakira sorted shapes into two different groups. Use geometric terms to describe how she sorted the shapes.

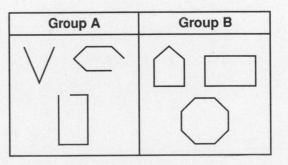

Group A	Group B

_____

_____

_____

Name _____

Polygons

Name each polygon. Then tell if it appears to be a regular polygon.

1.

_____

_____

2.

_____

_____

3. Name the polygon. Name the vertices.

_____

_____

4. Which polygon has eight sides?

A quadrilateral   **B** pentagon   **C** hexagon   **D** octagon

5. **Writing to Explain** Draw two regular polygons and two that are irregular. Use geometric terms to describe one characteristic of each type.

_____

_____

_____

Triangles

You can classify triangles by the lengths of their sides and the sizes of their angles.

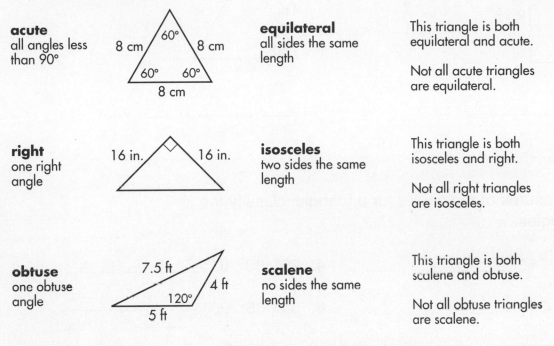

acute
all angles less than 90°

equilateral
all sides the same length

This triangle is both equilateral and acute.

Not all acute triangles are equilateral.

right
one right angle

isosceles
two sides the same length

This triangle is both isosceles and right.

Not all right triangles are isosceles.

obtuse
one obtuse angle

scalene
no sides the same length

This triangle is both scalene and obtuse.

Not all obtuse triangles are scalene.

Remember that the sum of the measures of the angles of a triangle is 180°.

Classify each triangle by its sides and then by its angles.

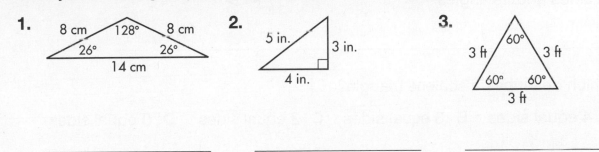

1.

2.

3.

_____

_____

_____

_____

_____

_____

Classify the following triangles based on the angles given.

4. 40°, 100°, 40° _____

5. 14°, 98°, 68° _____

6. 38°, 38°, 104° _____

Name _____

Triangles

Classify each triangle by its sides and then by its angles.

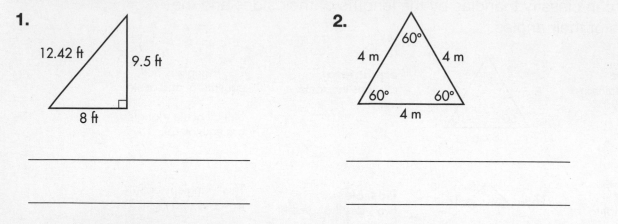

1.

2.

_____   _____

_____   _____

Given the measures of the angles for a triangle, classify the triangle by angles.

3. 47°, 62°, 71° _____   **4.** 29°, 90°, 61° _____

5. 75°, 75°, 30° _____   **6.** 54°, 36°, 90° _____

7. Judy bought a new tent for a camping trip. Look at the side of the tent with the opening to classify the triangle by its sides and its angles.

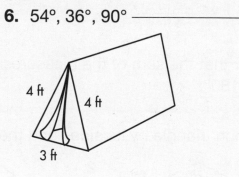

_____

8. Which describes a scalene triangle?

   A 4 equal sides   **B** 3 equal sides   **C** 2 equal sides   **D** 0 equal sides

9. The lengths of two sides of a triangle are 15 in. each. The third side measures 10 in. What type of triangle is this? Explain your answer using geometric terms.

_____

_____

Name _____

Properties of Quadrilaterals

Quadrilateral	Definition	Example
Parallelogram	A quadrilateral with both pairs of opposite sides parallel and equal in length	5 in. / 2 in. / 2 in. / 5 in.
Rectangle	A parallelogram with four right angles	5 ft / 2 ft / 2 ft / 5 ft
Rhombus	A parallelogram with all sides the same length	4 in. / 4 in. / 4 in. / 4 in.
Square	A rectangle with all sides the same length	1 ft / 1 ft / 1 ft / 1 ft
Trapezoid	A quadrilateral with only one pair of parallel sides	2 in. / 2 in. / 3 in. / 6 in.

Remember that the sum of the measures of the angles
of a quadrilateral is 360°.

Classify each quadrilateral. Be as specific as possible.

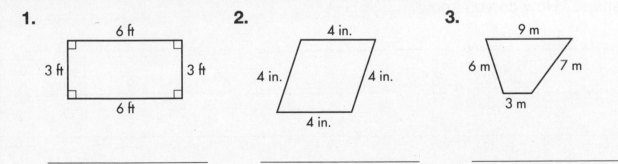

1. 6 ft / 3 ft / 3 ft / 6 ft

_____

2. 4 in. / 4 in. / 4 in. / 4 in.

_____

3. 9 m / 6 m / 7 m / 3 m

_____

4. How is a square similar to a rhombus? How is it different?

_____

_____

Name _____

Properties of Quadrilaterals

Classify each quadrilateral. Be as specific as possible.

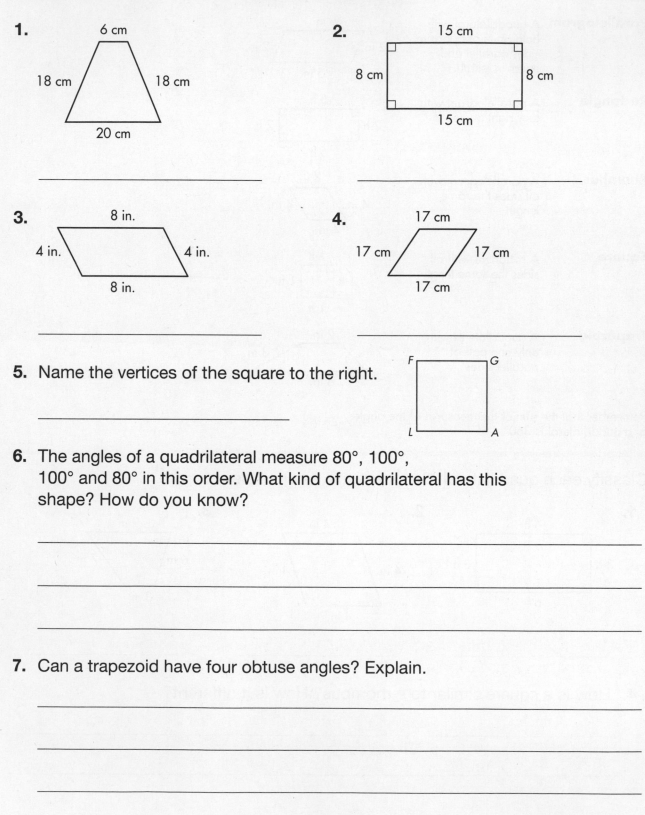

1.   6 cm
     18 cm   18 cm
          20 cm

_____

2.   15 cm
     8 cm   8 cm
          15 cm

_____

3.   8 in.
    4 in.   4 in.
       8 in.

_____

4.   17 cm
    17 cm   17 cm
       17 cm

_____

5. Name the vertices of the square to the right.

   F   G

   _____

   L   A

6. The angles of a quadrilateral measure 80°, 100°, 100° and 80° in this order. What kind of quadrilateral has this shape? How do you know?

   _____

   _____

   _____

7. Can a trapezoid have four obtuse angles? Explain.

   _____

   _____

Name _____

Special Quadrilaterals

Many special **quadrilaterals** have special properties.

A **trapezoid** has exactly one pair of parallel sides.

A **parallelogram** has two pairs of equal parallel sides.

A **rectangle** is a parallelogram with 4 right angles.

A **rhombus** is a parallelogram with 4 equal sides.

A **square** is a parallelogram with 4 right angles and 4 equal sides.

Identify each polygon. Describe each polygon by as many names as possible.

1. _____ _____

2. _____ _____

3. _____ _____ _____

4. _____ _____ _____

5. _____ _____ _____

6. _____

7. **Writing to Explain** Marvin says that all rhombuses are squares.
   Aretha says that all squares are rhombuses. Who is correct? Explain.

_____

_____

_____

Name _____

Special Quadrilaterals

In **1–6**, classify each polygon in as many ways as possible.

1. _____ _____ _____

2. _____ _____ _____

3. _____ _____ _____
_____

4. _____ _____ _____

5. _____ _____ _____

6. _____ _____ _____

7. Draw a quadrilateral with 1 pair of parallel sides. What special quadrilateral have you drawn?

_____

8. A parallelogram has one side that is 7 inches and one side that is 11 inches. What is the perimeter of the parallelogram?

_____

9. Which shows the most likely side lengths for a parallelogram?

  A 2, 2, 6, 2   **B** 2, 6, 2, 6   **C** 2, 2, 3, 6   **D** 2, 6, 6, 6

10. Writing to Explain What characteristics help you tell the difference between a rhombus and a rectangle? Explain.

_____

_____

_____

Classifying Quadrilaterals

How are special quadrilaterals related to each other?

This "family tree" shows how special quadrilaterals are related to each other.

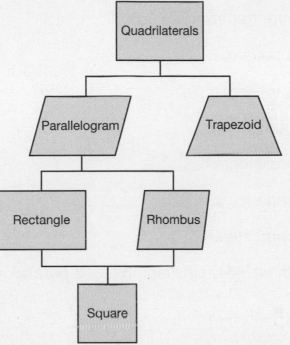

Tell whether each statement is true or false.

1. All squares are rhombuses. _____

2. Every trapezoid is a rectangle. _____

3. Squares are special parallelograms. _____

4. All quadrilaterals are squares. _____

5. All rhombuses are rectangles. _____

6. Every trapezoid is a quadrilateral. _____

7. Rhombuses are special parallelograms. _____

8. All rectangles are quadrilaterals. _____

Classifying Quadrilaterals

In **1–8**, tell whether each statement is true or false. Remember, for a statement to be true is has to be true in EVERY circumstance.

1. A rectangle is a quadrilateral. _____

2. All parallelograms are trapezoids. _____

3. A quadrilateral is a square. _____

4. A quadrilateral is a trapezoid. _____

5. A rhombus is a rectangle. _____

6. A trapezoid is a parallelogram. _____

7. A square is a rectangle. _____

8. A rectangle is a quadrilateral. _____

9. Which shows the most likely side lengths for a parallelogram?

   A 9, 4, 9, 4   **B** 9, 9, 9, 4   **C** 4, 4, 4, 9   **D** 4, 9, 9, 6

10. Draw 3 different quadrilaterals with 2 pairs of parallel sides. What are the names of the special quadrilaterals you have drawn?

    _____   _____   _____

11. A parallelogram has one side that is 9 millimeters and one side that is 13 millimeters. What is the perimeter of the parallelogram?

    _____

12. **Writing to Explain** What characteristics help you tell the difference between a parallelogram and a trapezoid? Explain.

    _____

Problem Solving: Make and Test Generalizations

Here is a generalization to be tested: any square can be cut in half through a diagonal. The result is always two isosceles triangles, each with a 90° angle.

Test one example of this generalization:

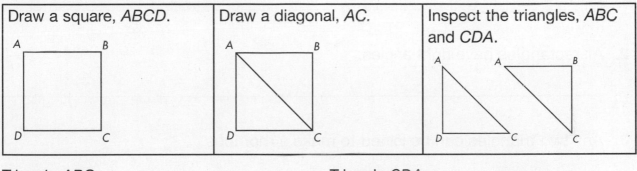

Draw a square, *ABCD*.	Draw a diagonal, *AC*.	Inspect the triangles, *ABC* and *CDA*.

Triangle *ABC*:

1. *AB = BC*   *All sides of a square are equal length.*

2. Angle *B* – 90°   *All angles of a square are 90°.*

Triangle *CDA*:

1. *CD = DA*   *All sides of a square are equal length.*

2. Angle *D* = 90°   *All angles of a square are 90°.*

Conclusion: Each triangle has two equal sides and contains a right angle. The generalization is true for the square *ABCD*.

Repeat for more squares. If for each square the conclusion is the same, the generalization appears to be correct.

Show that the triangles *ABC* and *CDA* are the same size and the same shape.

_____

_____

_____

_____

Problem Solving: Make and Test Generalizations

In **1** through **5**, test the generalization and state whether it appears to be correct or incorrect. If incorrect, give an example to support why.

1. All triangles have right angles.

_____

2. All rectangles have right angles.

_____

3. Any two triangles can be joined to make a rhombus.

_____

4. All rectangles can be cut in half vertically or horizontally to make two smaller rectangles that are the same size and same shape.

_____

5. Intersecting lines are also parallel.

_____

6. How many whole numbers have exactly three digits?
Hint: 999 is the greatest whole number with three digits.

   A 890   **B** 900   **C** 990   **D** 999

7. How can you show that a generalization is likely correct?

_____

_____

Name _____

Ordered Pairs

Locating a point on a coordinate grid

The ordered pair (5, 7) describes the location of Point *A*.

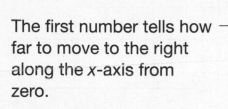

The first number tells how far to move to the right along the *x*-axis from zero.

This number is called the *x*-coordinate.

The second number tells how far to move up from the number on the *x*-axis.

This number is called the *y*-coordinate.

Locating a point from an ordered pair

Step 1: Start at zero.

Step 2: Move 5 spaces to the right.

Step 3: Move 7 spaces up.

The ordered pair for *B* is (8, 2).

The ordered pair for *C* is (6, 3).

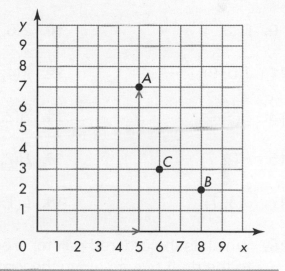

Name the point that is located by each ordered pair.

1. (7, 1) _____   **2.** (2, 6) _____

3. (0, 8) _____   **4.** (4, 3) _____

Write the ordered pair for each point.

5. *F* _____   **6.** *B* _____

7. *D* _____   **8.** *A* _____

9. Name two pairs of points that share the same *x*-coordinate.

_____

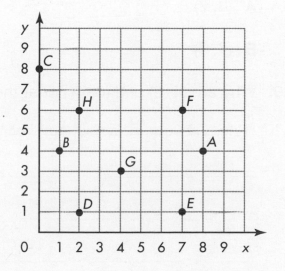

Ordered Pairs

Name the point that is located by each ordered pair.

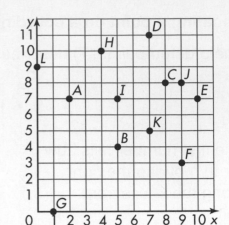

1. (9, 3) _____   **2.** (1, 0) _____

3. (7, 5) _____   **4.** (5, 7) _____

Write the ordered pair for each point.

5. D _____   **6.** C _____

7. E _____   **8.** L _____

Plot and label each point on the grid to the right.

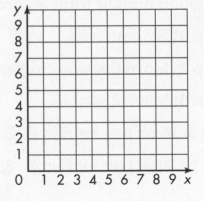

9. M(3, 4)   **10.** Z(6, 5)

11. T(0, 9)   **12.** X(4, 4)

13. P(3, 0)   **14.** A(2, 8)

15. H(7, 7)   **16.** B(2, 9)

17. J(3, 7)   **18.** L(1, 6)

19. Which is the ordered pair for a point that is 7 units
to the right of zero along the *x*-axis and 8 units above it?

A (8, 7)   **C** (1, 7)

B (7, 8)   **D** (1, 8)

20. Why are (4, 6) and (6, 4) not at the same point on a grid?

_____

_____

_____

_____

Distances on a Coordinate Plane

Jocelyn is going to plant carrots in rows. She is using a coordinate grid to help her arrange the rows.

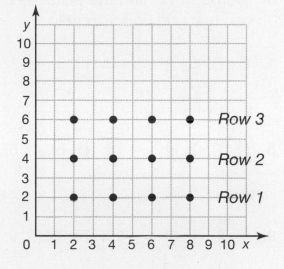

How long is each row?

Compare the ordered pairs
at each *end* of Row 1:   (2, **2**)
                                           (8, **2**)

The *y*-values are the same, so you know the row is horizontal.

The *x*-values are different. You can subtract the *x*-values to find the length of the row.
8 − 2 = 6

The length of Row 1 is 6 units.

How far away is the first row from the third row?

Compare the first ordered pairs from Rows 1 and 3:   (**2**, 2)
                                                          (**2**, 6)

The *x*-values are the same, so you know the distance is vertical. To find the distance between the first and third rows, subtract the *y*-values.
6 − 2 = 4

The distance between the first row and the third row is 4 units.

Find the distance between the ordered pairs.

1. (2, 2), (8, 2) _____ units   **2.** (3, 4), (3, 9) _____ units

3. (8, 4), (1, 4) _____ units   **4.** (1, 9), (9, 9) _____ units

5. (6, 1), (6, 5) _____ units   **6.** (1, 9), (1, 1) _____ units

7. If the ordered pairs (1, 4) and (9, 4) are connected to make a line, is the line vertical or horizontal? _____

Distances on a Coordinate Plane

For **1** through **12**, find the distance between the ordered pairs.
You can use grid paper to help.

1. (1, 7), (5, 7)   **2.** (3, 9), (3, 1)   **3.** (2, 6), (2, 0)   **4.** (12, 2), (1, 2)

_____   _____   _____   _____

5. (2, 7), (2, 8)   **6.** (1, 5), (5, 5)   **7.** (0, 1), (0, 3)   **8.** (15, 9), (4, 9)

_____   _____   _____   _____

9. (8, 4), (8, 8)   **10.** (7, 7), (7, 9)   **11.** (18, 7), (18, 13)   **12.** (16, 9), (16, 11)

_____   _____   _____   _____

13. On a map, a museum is located at (15, 17).
A library is located at (2, 17). How many units
away is the museum from the library?   _____

14. Matthew has two friends who live on the same block. On a map, Matthew's
house is located at (4, 2). Matthew's friend Josh lives at (4, 1). Their mutual
friend Kenny lives at (4, 8). Which friend lives farther from Matthew?

_____

15. On a map, a costume store is located at (18, 7). A general
store is located at (11, 7). How many units away is the costume
store from the general store?

A 6 units   **B** 7 units   **C** 8 units   **D** 9 units

16. On a map, John is standing at (11, 11). His friend Lucy is standing at (1, 11).
John took 10 steps to the right. Is he standing with Lucy now?

_____

_____

Problem Solving: Solve a Simpler Problem

Read	Rena's friend Emma is coming to visit her. Rena made her the map below showing Emma the way to her house.

How many blocks does Emma have to travel to get to Rena's house?

Plan & Solve	First, break the problem into simpler problems. **First problem:** Following the map, Emma has to travel north before turning east. How far does she have to travel north? *1 block north*
Plan & Solve	**Second problem:** Emma has to travel east before turning north. How far does she have to travel east? *5 blocks east*
Plan & Solve	**Third problem:** Emma now has to travel north to arrive at Rena's house. How far does she have to travel north? *3 blocks north*
Check	I can count the blocks and follow the route to check my calculations. Traveling 1 block north, 5 blocks east, and 3 blocks north will get Emma to Rena's house. Emma travels 9 blocks.

Use the information in the graph above to answer the following problems.

1. When her visit is over, Emma will use the same route to return back to her home. How many blocks will Emma have to travel for the entire trip to get to Rena's house and back home again?

_____

2. When Emma returns home, explain how she will travel.

_____

Problem Solving: Solve a Simpler Problem

For **1** and **2**, use the graph to the right.

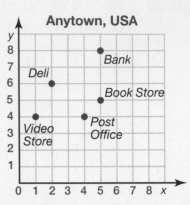

Anytown, USA

1. Mike is going from the video store to the deli to the post office. How many units does he travel?

   _____

2. Raja is going from the bank to the post office to the video store. Does he travel more units than Mike?

   _____

For **3** and **4** use the graph to the right.

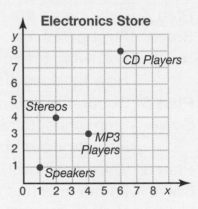

Electronics Store

3. Stephanie walked from the CD players to the MP3 players to the stereos. How many units did she walk?

   _____

4. Jule walked from the speakers to the stereos to the MP3 players. How many units did he walk?

   _____

5. Use the graph from Problems 1 and 2. Which location is the farthest from the bank?

   A Video Store   **B** Deli   **C** Post Office   **D** Book Store

6. Sal made a map of his neighborhood. According to his map, Sal's house is 6 units away from the grocery store. The grocery store is 5 units away from the coffee shop. The coffee shop is 1 unit from Sal's house. How is this possible?

   _____

   _____

Patterns and Graphing

Ron makes $5 every hour. A rule like this can be used to create a data table. The data can be plotted on a coordinate grid.

How to graph an rule:

Step 1:

Name three x-coordinates. Use the rule, substituting each x-coordinate to calculate each y-coordinate. Put the ordered pairs into the table.

Step 2:

Use grid paper. Choose an interval for each axis. Label and number the axes.

Choose the starting point and ending point for each axis.

Step 3:

Graph the data by using the coordinates for each set of data as a point. Connect all the points in a straight line. Title your graph.

STEP 1

$y = 5x$	
x-Hours	**y-Earnings**
0	0
1	5
2	10
3	15

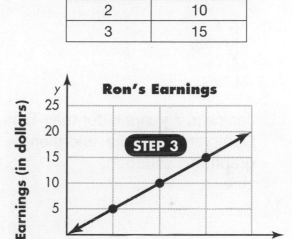

---

1. Graph the points from the table below to show the cost of buying harmonicas. Let x equal the number of harmonicas, and let y equal the cost of each harmonica. Harmonicas are available online for $3 each, plus a single shipping charge of $2.

$y = 3x + 2$	
x	**y**
1	5
2	8
3	11

Name _____

Patterns and Graphing

In **1** and **2** create a data table from the points plotted on the graph.

1.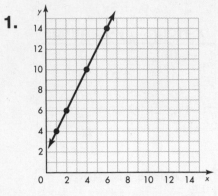

2.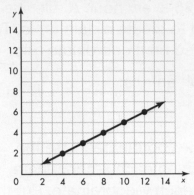

3. Janice is 7 years older than Tam. Complete the table, and then graph this situation.

Tam x (years)	Janice y (years)
2	9
4	
6	
8	

4. There are 4 cupcakes in every package. Complete the table, and then graph this situation.

x (number of packages)	y (number of cupcakes)
1	4
2	
3	
4	
5	

5. Tickets to the River Dell Middle School concert cost $6 apiece. Complete the table, and then graph this situation.

x (tickets sold)	y (money received)
1	$6
2	
3	
4	
5	

6. A graph includes the ordered pair (2, 4). Write two different rules that would be possible for this graph. Explain how you found your answer.

_____

_____

More Patterns and Graphing

Lila and Steve are saving money. Lila starts with no money and
Steve starts with $6. Each deposits $2 a day into a savings account.

Graph the relationship between the amount
of money each person saves. Let x = Lila's
money and y = Steve's money.

Lila and Steve's Savings

Choose 3 x-values.

Make a table of ordered pairs.

Graph the ordered pairs and draw a line.

Every x-value determines a y-value, so you
can find the value of y for each value of x.

	Lila	Steve
Start	0	6
Week 1	2	8
Week 2	4	10
Week 3	6	12

[Graph: Steve's Savings (in $) on vertical axis 1–14, Lila's Savings (in $) on horizontal axis 0–9, with a line through points (0,6), (2,8), (4,10), (6,12)]

For **1** through **3**, use the information below.

Rule for y_1: Add 3 to the x-value.
Rule for y_2: Add 6 to the x-value.

x	y_1	y_2
1	4	7
2		
3	6	
4		10
5	8	11
6	9	
7		

1. Find the missing information in the
table using the given rules.

_____

2. Find the values of y_1 and y_2
when x = 10.

_____

3. Graph the relationship between y_1
and y_2 on a coordinate grid.

_____

More Patterns and Graphing

For **1** and **2**, graph the corresponding coordinates of y_1 and y_2. Describe the relationship between the two sequences.

1.

Day	y_1	y_2
1	1	7
2	3	9
3	5	11
4	7	13

_____

_____

2.

Week	y_1	y_2
2	4	1
3	8	2
4	12	3
5	16	4

_____

_____

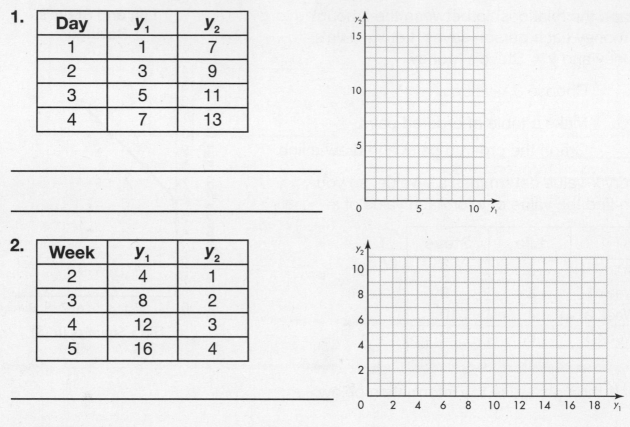

3. Dean is on a hike. The graph shows how far away he is from a camp site. How far away is he after 2 hours?

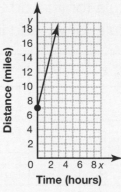

A 5 miles   **C** 15 miles

B 10 miles   **D** 20 miles

4. Ian gets $9 for each hour he works and $10 for each day he works. To find out how much he makes in a day, he made the equation $y = 9x + 10x$, where x is the number of hours he works. Explain why Ian's equation will not tell him how much he makes in a day.

_____

_____

_____

 P 16·5

Problem Solving: Work Backward

The movement of point A on a coordinate grid is described in the chart. What are the coordinates of A's starting location?

Time	Starting		1		2		Ending
Position	(x, y)		(9, 7)		(9, 5)		(6, 5)
Units/Direction		4 →		2 ↓		3 ←	

Read and Understand

What do you know?

The movements of point A and its final location

What are you trying to find?

A's starting location

Plan and Solve

Think: *Running the clock back in time from A's final location will place A back at its starting location.*

Since the clock is running in reverse, all directions will be reversed.

Solve the problem.

Time	Ending		2		1		Starting
Position	(6, 5)		(9, 5)		(9, 7)		(5, 7)
Units/Direction		3 →		2 ↑		4 ←	
Change		(6 + 3, 5)		(9, 5 + 2)		(9 − 4, 7)	

Write the answer in a complete sentence. A's starting location is (5, 7).

Look Back and Check

Is your answer correct?

Yes, (5 + 4 − 3, 7 − 2) is (6, 5).

Write the reverse for each of the following location changes.

1. 3 ↑ _____   2. 6 → _____   3. 4 ← _____   4. 2 ↓ _____

Write the new location for each of the following starting points and location changes.

5. (4, 3), 2 ↑ _____   6. (5, 3), 6 → _____   7. (8, 5), 3 ↓ _____

R 16·6

Problem Solving: Work Backward

Work backward to find each starting position.

1. **Starting** (x, y). _____
   4 units ➡ (14, 20)
   2 units ⬆ (14, 22)
   5 units ⬅ (9, 22) **Ending**

2. **Starting** (x, y). _____
   2 units ⬇ (5, 6)
   3 units ➡ (8, 6)
   1 unit ⬆ (8, 7) **Ending**

3. **Starting** (x, y). _____
   8 units ⬆ (5, 13)
   4 units ➡ (9, 13)
   6 units ➡ (15, 13) **Ending**

4. Martha must finish her math quiz in 35 minutes. She knows that there are 10 multiple-choice questions and 5 word problems. If each word problem takes her exactly 3 minutes to complete, how much time can she spend on each multiple-choice question?

_____

5. Kori arrived at school on time, at exactly 8:30 A.M. If it took him 15 minutes to walk to school, 10 minutes to eat breakfast, and 18 minutes to get ready, what time did he wake up this morning?

   A 7:37 A.M.   **C** 7:57 A.M.

   B 7:47 A.M.   **D** 8:07 A.M.

6. Jerry used his $100 gift certificate to go shopping. He bought pants for $25, a shirt for $15, and socks for $3. Then he bought a pair of shoes. Jerry still has $27 left. How much were the shoes that he bought? Explain how you know.

_____

_____

Name _____

Understanding Ratios

A ratio is a pair of numbers that compares two quantities.

Count to find the ratio of squares to circles.

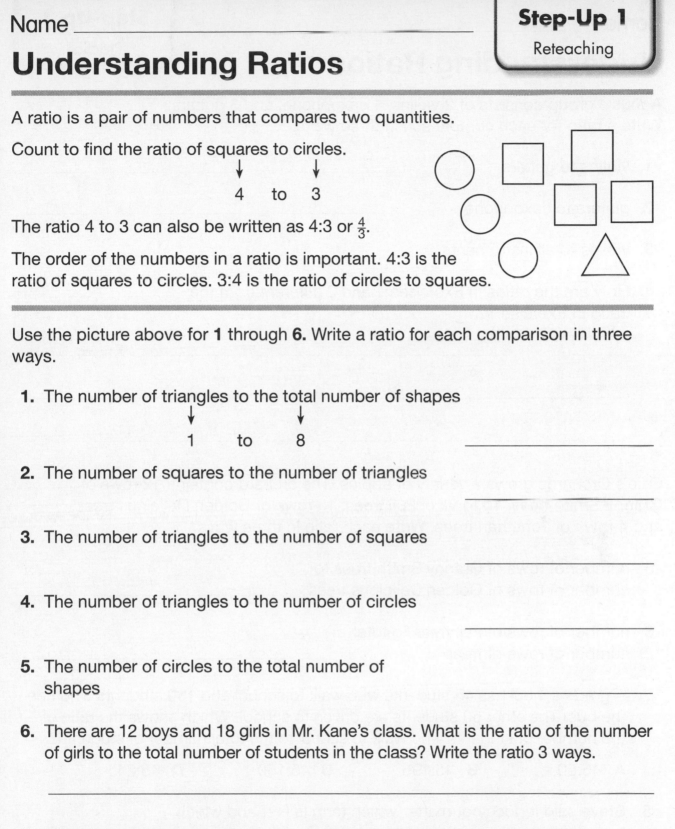

    ↓   ↓

    4   to   3

The ratio 4 to 3 can also be written as 4:3 or $\frac{4}{3}$.

The order of the numbers in a ratio is important. 4:3 is the ratio of squares to circles. 3:4 is the ratio of circles to squares.

Use the picture above for **1** through **6.** Write a ratio for each comparison in three ways.

1. The number of triangles to the total number of shapes

     ↓   ↓

    1   to   8   _____

2. The number of squares to the number of triangles

                                            _____

3. The number of triangles to the number of squares

                                            _____

4. The number of triangles to the number of circles

                                            _____

5. The number of circles to the total number of shapes

                                            _____

6. There are 12 boys and 18 girls in Mr. Kane's class. What is the ratio of the number of girls to the total number of students in the class? Write the ratio 3 ways.

_____

7. **Writing to Explain** There are 9 cats and 17 dogs at an animal hospital. Use this fact to write two ratios and explain what each means.

_____

Understanding Ratios

A music group consists of 2 violins, 1 saxophone, and 3 guitars.
Write a ratio for each comparison in three ways.

1. violins to guitars _____

2. guitars to saxophone _____

3. violins to all instruments _____

4. How are the ratios in Exercises 1 and 2 different from the ratio in Exercise 3?

_____

_____

_____

Ollie's Orchards grows a variety of apples. The orchard contains 12 rows of Granny Smith trees, 10 rows of Fuji trees, 15 rows of Golden Delicious trees, and 4 rows of Jonathan trees. Write each ratio in three ways.

5. number of rows of Granny Smith trees to
number of rows of Golden Delicious trees _____

6. number of rows of Fuji trees to total
number of rows of trees _____

7. A grade school has 45 students who walk to school and 150 students who ride the bus. The other 50 students are driven to school. Which shows the ratio of the number of students who walk to school to the total number of students?

A 45:50   **B** 45:195   **C** 45:150   **D** 45:245

8. Steve said it does not matter which term is first and which term is second in a ratio. Is he correct? Explain.

_____

_____

Name _____

Understanding Rates and Unit Rates

A rate is a ratio in which the two terms are measured in different units.

Example: 18 bracelets for 3 girls.
18 bracelets
3 girls

In a unit rate, the second number is 1.

Example: 6 bracelets for 1 girl.
6 bracelets
1 girl

Remember that the fraction bar shows division.
If you know a rate, you can divide to find the unit rate.

Example: 17 goals in 5 games is written as $\frac{17 \text{ goals}}{5 \text{ games}}$.

$$5\overline{)17.0}^{\,3.4}$$ The unit rate is 3.4 goals per game. (Per means "for each.")

Write the rate and the unit rate.

1. 35 flowers for 5 vases

_____

2. 24 games in 8 weeks

_____

3. 144 pencils in 12 packages

_____

4. 252 students in 9 classes

_____

5. $13.20 for 6 pounds

_____

6. 44 minutes for 8 pages

_____

7. If a car travels 350 miles in 5 hours, what is its rate per hour?

_____

8. Estimation Bare root plum trees are on sale at 3 for $40. To the nearest dollar, what is the cost per tree?

_____

Name _____

Understanding Rates and Unit Rates

Write the rate and the unit rate.

1. 42 bricks laid in 2 hours

_____

2. 25 points scored in 4 quarters

_____

3. 240 chairs in 15 rows

_____

4. 72 plants in 9 square feet

_____

5. 420 miles on 14 gallons

_____

6. $6.50 for 10 pounds

_____

7. Estimation Over 5 days, 8,208 people visited an amusement park. About how many people visited the park per day?

_____

8. Explain how you could convert a rate of 18,000 miles per hour to miles per second.

_____

_____

9. Dimitri makes 6 bookcases in 8 days. What is his unit rate?

_____

10. A space shuttle orbits Earth 1 time in 90 minutes. How many times does it orbit Earth in 6 hours?

_____

11. Which is the unit rate for 39 people in 13 vans?

   A 39 people per van   **C** 13 vans per person

   B 13 people per van   **D** 3 people per van

Name _____

Equal Ratios and Proportions

You can find equal ratios just like you find equivalent fractions.

Find ratios equal to $\frac{30}{40}$.

Multiply both terms by the same number.

$\frac{30 \times 2}{40 \times 2} = \frac{60}{80}$

Divide both terms by the same number. To find the simplest form ratio, divide by the greatest common factor (GCF) of the two numbers.

The GCF of 30 and 40 is 10.

$\frac{30 \div 10}{40 \div 10} = \frac{3}{4}$

Two equal ratios form a proportion. The units must be the same in both ratios.

Do the ratios 24 ft:16 seconds and 36 ft:24 seconds form a proportion?

First check the units.

Both ratios compare feet to seconds, so the units are the same.

Then write each ratio in simplest form.

$\frac{24 \text{ ft}}{16 \text{ sec}} = \frac{3 \text{ ft}}{2 \text{ sec}}$

$\frac{36 \text{ ft}}{24 \text{ sec}} = \frac{3 \text{ ft}}{2 \text{ sec}}$

Compare the simplest form ratios. They are the same, so the ratios form a proportion.

Write three ratios that are equal to the ratio given.

1. $\frac{3}{5}$ _____

2. $\frac{4}{8}$ _____

3. $\frac{6}{18}$ _____

4. 8:10 _____

5. 6:8 _____

6. 50:60 _____

7. 4 to 6

8. 8 to 9

9. 5 to 25

_____ _____ _____

Write the ratios in simplest form.

10. $\frac{10}{15}$ _____

11. 21 to 14 _____

12. 30:60 _____

Write = if the ratios form a proportion; if they do not form a proportion, write ≠.

13. $\frac{15}{18}, \frac{10}{12}$ _____

14. 20:24, 30:34 _____

15. 16 to 20, 28 to 35 _____

16. Alain says that the ratios 3:5 and 2:10 are equal. Is he correct? Explain.

_____

Name _____

Equal Ratios and Proportions

Write three ratios that are equal to the ratio given.

1. $\frac{40}{50}$ _____ **2.** $\frac{2}{3}$ _____ **3.** $\frac{75}{100}$ _____

4. 21 to 18 _____ **5.** 5 to 4 _____ **6.** 1 to 3 _____

7. 14:16 _____ **8.** 2:4 _____ **9.** 20:50 _____

Write = if the ratios form a proportion; if they do not form a proportion, write ≠.

10. 3:12, 9:36 _____ **11.** $\frac{14}{16}, \frac{7}{4}$ _____ **12.** 4 to 20, 1 to 4 _____

Find the number that makes the ratios equivalent.

13. $\frac{8}{9}$ = _____ /36 **14.** 15:18 = 5: _____ **15.** _____ to 7 = 9 to 21

Write the ratios in simplest form.

16. $\frac{42}{28}$ _____ **17.** 28 to 48 _____ **18.** 25:75 _____

19. $\frac{35}{25}$ _____ **20.** 90 to 45 _____ **21.** 10:40 _____

22. Tell why you cannot multiply or divide by zero to find equal ratios.

_____

23. Is the ratio of length to width for these two rectangles proportional? Tell how you know.

14 in.   21 in.

7 in.   15 in.

_____

_____

24. Which value for x would make the ratios equivalent?

$\frac{3}{8} = \frac{x}{32}$

A $x = 4$ **B** $x = 6$ **C** $x = 8$ **D** $x = 12$

Name _____

Using Ratio Tables

A ratio table showing equal ratios can be used to solve a proportion.

Don uses 11 skeins of yarn to make 4 scarves. How many scarves can he make from 66 skeins of yarn?

Write a proportion. Use *x* for the number of scarves.

$$\frac{4 \text{ scarves}}{11 \text{ skeins}} = \frac{x \text{ scarves}}{66 \text{ skeins}}$$

Make a ratio table. Multiply or divide to find equal ratios. Find ratios equivalent to $\frac{4}{11}$ by multiplying both terms of the ratio by the same number until you find 66 skeins.

Number of scarves	4	8	12	16	20	24
Number of skeins	11	22	33	44	55	66

$$\frac{4 \text{ scarves}}{11 \text{ skeins}} = \frac{24 \text{ scarves}}{66 \text{ skeins}}$$

So, Don can make 24 scarves from 66 skeins of yarn.

Answer the question and complete each ratio table.

1. $\dfrac{\$25}{\boxed{} \text{ min}} = \dfrac{\$200}{1,000 \text{ min}}$

Number of dollars	200	100	50	25
Number of minutes	1,000			

2. $\dfrac{\boxed{} \text{ batteries}}{9 \text{ flashlights}} = \dfrac{12 \text{ batteries}}{3 \text{ flashlights}}$

Number of batteries				
Number of flashlights				

3. $\dfrac{\boxed{} \text{ yd}}{800 \text{ h}} = \dfrac{9 \text{ yd}}{8 \text{ h}}$

Number of _____				
Number of _____				

4. $\dfrac{4 \text{ carts}}{24 \text{ horses}} = \dfrac{\boxed{} \text{ carts}}{96 \text{ horses}}$

Number of _____				
Number of _____				

5. Katie was practicing her free throws. She shot 9 times and made 7 baskets. At this rate, how many times will she need to shoot to make 35 baskets?

_____

6. Raul said that he can use the same ratio table to solve the two proportions below. Do you agree or disagree with Raul?

$\dfrac{8 \text{ cows}}{2 \text{ pigs}} = \dfrac{c \text{ cows}}{10 \text{ pigs}}$ $\dfrac{2 \text{ pigs}}{8 \text{ cows}} = \dfrac{10 \text{ pigs}}{c \text{ cows}}$

_____

    5

Name _____

Using Ratio Tables

Complete the ratio table. Add columns if needed.

1. $\dfrac{3 \text{ hops}}{7 \text{ jumps}} = \dfrac{\boxed{} \text{ hops}}{21 \text{ jumps}}$

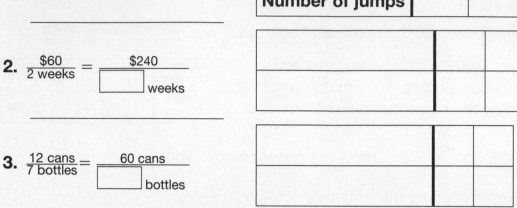

Number of hops		
Number of jumps		

2. $\dfrac{\$60}{2 \text{ weeks}} = \dfrac{\$240}{\boxed{} \text{ weeks}}$

3. $\dfrac{12 \text{ cans}}{7 \text{ bottles}} = \dfrac{60 \text{ cans}}{\boxed{} \text{ bottles}}$

4. How many cups of loam are needed to make 66 c of potting soil? _____

5. How many cups of humus are needed to make 11 c of potting soil? _____

6. Sasha uses 58 c of loam to make potting soil. How many cups of humus did she use? _____

Potting Soil for Ferns (Makes 22 c)

6 c sand
6 c loam
6 c peat moss
3 c humus
1 c dried cow manure

7. It takes Renee 8 h to make 7 carvings. At this rate, how many hours will it take him to make 63 carvings?

A $7\frac{7}{8}$ h

B 9 h

C 56 h

D 72 h

8. Find three sets of values for x and y to make $\dfrac{x \text{ mi}}{y \text{ min}} = \dfrac{4 \text{ mi}}{32 \text{ min}}$ a proportion. Explain how you found the values.

_____

_____

Name _____

Comparing Rates

Use unit rates to compare two rates that have the same units of measurement.

Daniel painted 9 planks in 6 minutes. Meredith painted 22 planks in 11 minutes. Who painted at a faster rate? Write each rate as a unit rate.

Daniel's rate: $\frac{9 \text{ planks}}{6 \text{ min}}$

$\frac{= 9 \text{ planks} \div 6}{6 \text{ min} \div 6} = \frac{1.5 \text{ planks}}{1 \text{ min}}$

Meredith's rate: $\frac{22 \text{ planks}}{11 \text{ min}}$

$\frac{= 22 \text{ planks} \div 11}{11 \text{ min} \div 11} = \frac{2 \text{ planks}}{1 \text{ min}}$

Since 2 is greater than 1.5, Meredith is the faster painter. The faster rate is 22 planks in 11 min.

Find each unit rate and determine which rate is greater.

1. 51 hits on Jon's website in 3 h or 64 hits on Shana's website in 4 h

_____

_____

2. 352 mi on 16 gal or 240 mi on 10 gal

_____

3. 90 breaths in 6 min or 126 breaths in 9 min

_____

Find each unit price and determine which is a better buy.

4. 20 gallons of gas for $66.00 or 25 gallons of gas for $81.25

_____

5. **Writing to Explain** Evan and Li danced in a charity fundraiser. Evan raised $275 when he danced for 5 hours. Li raised $376 when she danced for 8 hours. Which dancer earned more for each hour danced? Explain how you found your answer.

_____

Comparing Rates

Find each unit rate and determine which rate is greater.

1. 250 mi per 10 gal or 460 mi per 20 gal

_____

2. 500 words in 10 min or 2,475 words in 45 min

_____

3. 6 in. of rain in 4 h or 16 in. of rain in 10 h

_____

Find each unit price and determine which is a better buy.

4. 1 lb of apples for $2.25 or 3 lb of apples for $5.76

_____

5. 16 bungee cords for $20.00 or 20 bungee cords for $22.00

_____

6. 5 oz of insect repellant for $6.95 or 14 oz of insect repellant for $19.60

_____

7. Fran earns $75.60 for each 7-h shift that she works. Which shift pays a higher hourly wage than the wage Fran earns?

A $60.30 for a 6-h shift   **C** $36.30 for a 3-h shift

B $80.00 for an 8-h shift   **D** $40.40 for a 4-h shift

8. Sue says that 4 towels for $17 is a better buy than 2 towels for $9. She found her answer by doubling the terms in the ratio $\frac{9}{2}$ and comparing the first terms in the ratios. Is she correct?

_____

_____

Name _____

Multiplying with Zeros in the Product

When you multiply decimals, sometimes your product does not have enough places for the decimal point. You will need to insert one or more zeros into your product to serve as placeholders.

Gabriella drove 0.3 mile yesterday. Sam drove 0.2 times as far as Gabriella. How many miles did Sam drive?

A grid can help you visualize the product.

The squares that are shaded show 0.3. The squares with a dot show 0.2.

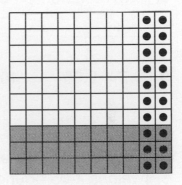

The squares that are both shaded and dotted show the product. $0.2 \times 0.3 = 6$ hundredths. To write this decimal correctly, you must add a zero in the tenths place as a placeholder.

        6 hundredths = 0.06

You can also count the number of decimal places in both factors. The total number of decimal places equals the number of decimal places in your product.

    0.3 1 decimal place
  × 0.2 1 decimal place
    0.6 2 decimal places

Since you need 2 decimal places in your product and you have only one digit in your product, you need to add a zero to the left of the 6 as a placeholder. The product then correctly becomes 0.06.

In questions **1–4**, find each product.

1. 0.3
  ×0.42

2. 4.01
  ×0.02

3. 0.16
  ×0.5

4. 7.06
  ×0.01

If $0.4 \times 0.2 = 0.08$, what is the value of n in the following equations?

5. $0.4 \times n = 0.008$ _____

6. $0.4 \times n = 0.0008$ _____

7. $n \times 0.2 = 0.00008$ _____

Name _____

Multiplying with Zeros in the Product

Find each product.

1.	0.3	2.	0.4	3.	5.04	4.	0.13
	× 0.2		× 0.17		× 0.02		× 0.05

5. 0.97 × 0.05   **6.** 8.02 × 0.002   **7.** 1.04 × 0.3   **8.** 1.06 × 0.08

_____   _____   _____   _____

9. 0.7 × 2.05   **10.** 0.80 × 0.02   **11.** 0.09 × 5.01   **12.** 4.05 × 0.012

_____   _____   _____   _____

13. The fifth-grade math textbook weighs 2.05 pounds. There are 85 students taking math at the Ladd School. What is the total weight of all the math textbooks?

_____

14. The Changs received a delivery of fuel oil totaling 35.00 gallons. The oil cost $3.05 per gallon. What did the Changs pay for the delivery?

_____

15. Mia spends 1.5 hours in the computer lab each afternoon. If the computer uses 0.09 kilowatt of electricity per hour, how many kilowatt hours does Mia use each afternoon?

A 13.50   **B** 1.35   **C** 0.135   **D** 0.0135

16. Is the product of 0.04 × 0.04 the same as the product of 0.4 × 0.004? Explain.

_____

_____

_____

_____

Name _____

Greatest Common Factor

The greatest number that divides into two numbers is the greatest common factor (GCF) of the two numbers. Here are two ways to find the GCF of 16 and 40.

List the Factors

Step 1: List the factors of each number.

16: 1, 2, 4, 8, 16

40: 1, 2, 4, 5, 8, 10, 20, 40

Step 2: Circle the factors that are common to both numbers.

16: 1, ②④⑧ 16

40: 1, ②④ 5, ⑧ 10, 20, 40

Step 3: Choose the greatest factor that is common to both numbers. 2, 4 and 8 are common factors, but 8 is greatest.

The GCF is 8.

Use Prime Factorization

Step 1: Write the prime factorization of each number.

16: 2 × 2 × 2 × 2

40: 2 × 2 × 2 × 5

Step 2: Circle the prime factors that the numbers have in common.

16: ②×②×②× 2

40: ②×②×②× 5

Step 3: Multiply the common factors.

2 × 2 × 2 = 8   The GCF is 8.

Find the GCF for each set of numbers.

1. 10, 90 _____   2. 4, 20 _____   3. 18, 30 _____

4. 36, 63 _____   5. 36, 42 _____   6. 14, 28 _____

7. Name two numbers that have a greatest common factor of 8.

_____

8. Al's garden is 18 feet long and 30 feet wide. He wants to put fence posts the same distance apart along both the length and width of the fence. What is the greatest distance apart he can put the fence posts?

_____

  5

Name _____

Greatest Common Factor

Find the GCF for each set of numbers.

1. 36, 48 _____   **2.** 20, 24 _____   **3.** 63, 84 _____

4. 48, 100 _____   **5.** 18, 130 _____   **6.** 90, 95 _____

7. Name three pairs of numbers that have 5 as their greatest common factor. Use each number only once in your answer.

_____

8. The bake-sale committee divided each type of item evenly onto plates, so that every plate contained only one type of item and every plate had exactly the same number of items with no leftovers. What is the maximum number of items that could have been placed on each plate?

Bake Sale Donations	
Muffins	96
Bread sticks	48
Rolls	84

_____

9. Using this system, how many plates of rolls could the bake-sale committee make? _____

10. Using this system, how many plates of muffins could the bake-sale committee make? _____

11. Which of the following pairs of numbers is correctly listed with its greatest common factor?

   A 20, 24; GCF: 4   **C** 4, 6; GCF: 24

   B 50, 100; GCF: 10   **D** 15, 20; GCF: 35

12. Writing to Explain Explain one method of finding the greatest common factor of 48 and 84.

_____

_____

_____

_____

Name _____

Using Expressions to Describe Patterns

You can write an expression to describe the pattern in an input/output table.

Look at the first input and output values in the table.

Ask Yourself: What do I need to do to the input 11 to get the output 6? You might need to add, subtract, multiply, divide, or perform more than one operation.

INPUT	OUTPUT
11	6
12	7
13	8
15	★
20	★

In this table, you can subtract 5 from 11 to get 6. Check the input and output values for 12 and 13.

$12 - 5 = 7$ $13 - 5 = 8$

The pattern is true for all of the values in the table. So, the pattern is subtract 5. You can write the expression $x - 5$ to describe the pattern.

Substitute input values for the variable x to get the output values.

Find the output values for 15 and 20.   _____

The input/output table shows how much Rey pays for toys. Use the input/output table for **1** through **4**.

1. If Rey buys 15 toys, what is the cost?   _____

2. If Rey pays $45, how many toys did he buy?   _____

3. Write an expression to describe the output pattern if the input is the variable t.   _____

INPUT	OUTPUT
6	18
7	21
8	24
9	27

4. What inputs and outputs should be added to the table for 20 toys?   _____

5. **Writing to Explain** Sally says that the expression $2x$ describes the input/output table. Explain why Sally's expression is correct or incorrect.

INPUT	2	3	4	5
OUTPUT	4	5	6	7

_____

_____

Name _____

Using Expressions to Describe Patterns

Use this table for **1** through **4**.

Total Cups in Boxes	18	36	54	66	72	84
Total Number of Boxes	3	6	9	☐	☐	☐

1. How many boxes are needed for 66, 72, and 84 cups? _____

2. How many cups will be in 30 boxes? _____

3. Write an algebraic expression that explains the relationship between the input (total cups in boxes) and output values (total number of boxes) if the variable c is the input. _____

4. Max thinks he needs 25 boxes to pack 144 cups. Is Max correct? Explain.

_____

_____

5. Ted is using seashells to make necklaces. Each necklace has 7 shells. Make an input/output table that shows the number of shells used for 10, 15, 20, and 25 necklaces. Write an algebraic expression that explains the relationship between the input and output values.

Use this table for **6** and **7**.

Large White Butterfly Wing Beats					
Number of seconds	1	2	3	4	5
Number of beats	12	24	36	48	60

6. What algebraic expression shows the number of wing beats for a chosen number of seconds?

    A $60 + x$　　　　**B** $x \div 12$　　　　**C** $12 \div x$　　　　**D** $12x$

7. How many times will a large white butterfly beat its wings in 12 seconds?

    A 144　　　　　**B** 120　　　　　**C** 84　　　　　**D** 72

Commutative Properties	Associative Properties
You can add or multiply numbers in any order and the sum or product will be the same.	You can group numbers differently. It will not affect the sum or product.
Examples: $10 + 5 + 3 = 5 + 3 + 10 = 18$ $7 \times 5 = 5 \times 7 = 35$	**Examples:** $2 + (7 + 6) = (2 + 7) + 6 = 15$ $(4 \times 5) \times 8 = 4 \times (5 \times 8) = 160$
Identity Properties You can add 0 to a number or multiply it by 1 and not change the value of the number. **Examples:** $17 + 0 = 17$ $45 \times 1 = 45$	**Multiplication Property of Zero** If you multiply a number by 0, the product will always be 0. **Example:** $12 \times 0 = 0$

Find each missing number. Tell what property or properties are shown.

1. $9 \times 14 = 14 \times$ _____

_____

2. _____ $\times 99 = 99$

_____

3. $(3 + 4) + 91 = 3 + ($ _____ $+ 91)$

_____

4. $987 +$ _____ $= 987$

_____

5. What is the product of any number, x, multiplied by 1? Explain how you know.

_____

_____

Name _____

Properties of Operations

Find each missing number. Tell what property or properties are shown.

1. $(45 + \underline{\hspace{1cm}}) + 2 + 7 = 45 + (14 + 2) + 7$

_____

2. $8 + 51 + 12 = \underline{\hspace{1cm}} + 12 + 51$

_____

3. $(8 \times \underline{\hspace{1cm}}) \times 16 = 8 \times (9 \times 16)$

_____

4. $\underline{\hspace{1cm}} + 0 = 34$

_____

5. $12 \times 5 = 5 \times \underline{\hspace{1cm}}$

_____

6. $1 \times \underline{\hspace{1cm}} = 288$

_____

7. Write a number sentence that shows why the Associative Property does not work with subtraction.

_____

8. Which property is shown in $(23 \times 5) \times 31 \times 7 = 23 \times (5 \times 31) \times 7$?

A Commutative Property of Multiplication   **C** Identity Property of Multiplication

B Associative Property of Multiplication   **D** Associative Property of Addition

9. Explain why you do not have to do any computing to solve $75 \times 0 \times (13 + 7)$.

_____

_____

Surface Area

The **surface area** of a rectangular prism is the sum of the areas of all of its faces.

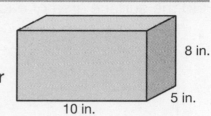
8 in.
5 in.
10 in.

Monica has a wood block. She wants to paint it. In order to know how much paint to buy, Monica needs to find the surface area of the block.

If you could "unfold" this block, its net would look like this:

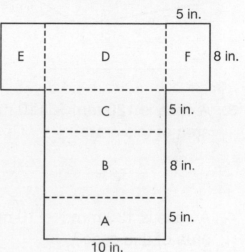

You can find the area of each rectangular face by multiplying the base times the height.

area of A = 10 × 5 = 50
area of B = 10 × 8 = 80
area of C = 10 × 5 = 50
area of D = 10 × 8 = 80
area of E = 8 × 5 = 40
area of F = 8 × 5 = 40

Adding all the areas together will give the total surface area.

50 + 80 + 50 + 80 + 40 + 40 = 340 in²

In **1** through **3**, find the surface area of each figure.

1.
5 cm
5 cm
5 cm

2.
2 mm
6 mm
12 mm

3.
11 ft
4 ft
6 ft

_____   _____   _____

4. Sapna wants to decorate the outside of this box. What is the total area that her decorations could cover?

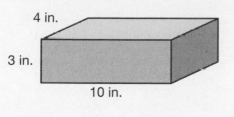
4 in.
3 in.
10 in.

_____

Name _____

Surface Area

Find the surface area of each rectangular prism.

1.

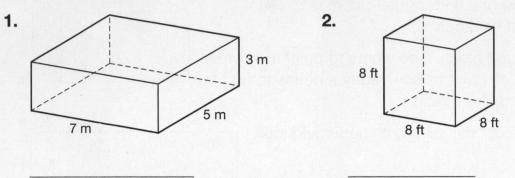

3 m

5 m

7 m

2.

8 ft

8 ft   8 ft

_____   _____

3. A case is 120 mm × 110 mm × 4 mm. What is the surface area of this crate?

_____

4. A case is 130 mm × 110 mm × 10 mm. What is the surface area of this case?

_____

5. Find the surface area of a cereal box that is 11 inches high, 9 inches long, and 2 inches wide. If helpful, draw a net of the box.

_____

6. What is the surface area of a rectangular prism with the dimensions 5 in. × 6 in. × 10 in.?

A 280 in²   **B** 230 in²   **C** 220 in²   **D** 180 in²

7. Give an example of when you would use the formula for finding the surface area of a rectangular prism.

_____

_____

_____

   5